SIX SECRETS
TO **YOUR**
SUCCESS!

HOMESCHOOL

REBECA CRUZ

Copyright © 2021 by Rebeca Cruz.

All rights reserved. This book or any portion thereof may not be reproduced or used in any manner whatsoever without the express written permission of the publisher except for the use of brief quotations in a book review.

Publishing Services provided by Paper Raven Books

Printed in the United States of America

First Printing, 2021

Paperback ISBN= 978-1-7361477-0-2
Hardback ISBN= 978-1-7361477-1-9

MY CHILDREN SPEAK

The best gift my mom ever gave me was the decision she made to homeschool me. I wouldn't trade my homeschool years for anything in the world. Everything I am today is because of the sacrifice my mom made to stay home and homeschool.

~Melody Cruz Machado

Growing up in a homeschool household has taught me three things: family first, be the difference, and love God. I don't believe I would have these same convictions if I was raised differently.

~Jason O. Cruz

Being homeschooled is not waking up late, not doing school in your pajamas, or not being socialized. My mother taught me how to learn what really matters, how to work hard to achieve my dreams, and how to breathe in the little moments. Now, that's a homeschooler!

~Melanie G. Cruz

For Melody, Jason, and Melanie
You are the reason I do what I do best!
I am honored to be your mom.
For Obed, my husband
Thank you for believing in me,
for supporting me, and for loving me.

TABLE OF CONTENTS

Introduction: When You Don't Know How — 1

Unit 1: Homeschool as a Lifestyle — 5
- Setting Up Space in the House — 8
- Homeschool with the End in Mind — 11
- Vision — 13
- Plan — 15
- Mission Board — 15
- Priority and Commitment — 16
- Put Your Children First — 17
- Family Calendar — 20
- Planning Makes Things Better — 21
- Creating a Family Dynamic with Your Spouse — 25
- Creating a Family Dynamic with Your Children — 30
- Creating a Family Dynamic with Grandparents and Other Family Members — 37

Unit 2: Curriculum — 43
- The "Later" Approach — 49
- The Importance of a Support Group — 51
- Extracurricular Activities — 54
- Certified Curriculums and Umbrella Schools — 57

- How to Make a Portfolio — 60
  - ◊ Traditional Portfolio — 60
  - ◊ Digital or Online Portfolio — 62
- Evaluations, Testing, and Laws of Homeschooling — 63
- Finding Your Children's Passion and Career Interest — 67
- Shadowing and Volunteering — 71

Unit 3: Children's Daily Schedules and Routines — 75
- Preschool Schedule — 82
- Elementary School Schedule — 83
- Middle School and High School Schedule — 84
- Rewards — 85
- Chore Example List — 86

Unit 4: Character Building — 89

Unit 5: How to Take Care of What Matters Most (YOU) — 101
- Empowering Your Soul — 104
  - ◊ Spiritual Life — 104
  - ◊ God's Word — 106
  - ◊ Bible Study — 107
  - ◊ Prayer Journal — 109
  - ◊ Prayer Partners — 110
  - ◊ Prayer Walk — 110
  - ◊ Talk to God All Day — 111
  - ◊ Mom Prayer Time — 112

- Praise ... 112
  - ◊ Play Praise ... 113
  - ◊ Physical Praise ... 114
  - ◊ Praise with Instruments ... 114
- Taking Care of Your Body ... 115
  - ◊ Personal Appointments ... 118
  - ◊ Drink Water ... 118
  - ◊ Take Your Vitamins ... 118
  - ◊ Rest ... 118
- Beautify Yourself ... 120
- Eating Healthy ... 121
- Exercise ... 124
- Expand Your Mind ... 126
- Have Fun ... 128

Unit 6: How to Keep It All Together ... 133
- Personal Calendar ... 134
- Mom's Schedule ... 135
- House Chores ... 137
- Family Menu ... 138
- Grocery List ... 140
- Bills and Budget Spreadsheet ... 143
- Filing System ... 146
- To-Do List ... 147
- Challenges: Taking the Risk ... 148

How to Use the "Action Steps" Pages

I believe that by the time you read this book, you will have a new, improved, and successful homeschool. Applying the concepts and recommendations presented in this book will allow you to have the positive results you want and make your job more doable as a homeschool parent. The "Action Steps" page is designed to help you and make things easier for you. On this page, you will be able to write down your reflections, notes, and tools learned in each section so you can make things happen.

I desire to show you practical techniques that will transform your homeschooling and give you insight into how it can be done. By the time you finish reading this book, you will have your own set of guidelines written on the "Action Steps" pages and acquired the proper tools to take action to do it yourself.

Introduction

WHEN YOU DON'T KNOW HOW

I knew exactly the type of family I wanted to create. As I sat in the back porch of my home, staring at the blue sky on a hot, late summer afternoon, I felt overwhelmed with anxiety and afraid of the unknown. I was insecure about teaching my children, worried about criticism from family and friends, and uneasy about financial adjustments that would result from leaving my job of over 15 years (which I loved) and becoming codependent with my husband in an independent society. All of this to venture into a new lifestyle called homeschooling. It was more than I could handle.

I realized I was facing an awkward situation, but just like any other obstacle in my life, I had to rise to and overcome the challenge. I understood that this new lifestyle wasn't going to come about magically. I needed to find the proper tools, identify my weaknesses and strengths, find the "why," and conquer what appeared to be my problem.

Then came the hard work, sacrifices, adjustments, modifications, adaptations, and transitions. That was not the end of the story but the beginning of a new lifestyle ready to unfold. My hope is that my success story will give you hope and show you what you can obtain when you are convinced and determined to act and think outside of the box for the sake of providing the best for your children.

My husband and I, although like-minded about religious beliefs, education, politics, marriage, and family commitment, were brought up differently and with different value systems. One unwavering aspect in our lives on which we both agree 100% of the time is child-rearing, because we understand that parenting is a higher calling. We both want the best for our children. Therefore, having my husband's support throughout all these changes made my new career easy to embrace.

It all started many years ago. We married young, and like most other couples, finishing our careers, buying our dream home, and traveling were all in the plans. Children would have to wait because even then, we both realized the work and commitment that it would take, and we wanted to do it right from the start. The years passed and all of those dreams became a reality. With hard work, determination, and goal setting, we were able to accomplish every one of those dreams. Now we were ready for a family, but the "now" became a long and disheartening period in my life. Weeks turned into months and months into years, and my chances of conceiving were becoming scarce. What I thought

Introduction: When You Don't Know How

was the most natural thing in the world—to have a family—was not so natural for me. And the reality of never having children was becoming something I had to face. Appointments, blood tests, treatments were the norm for me. Every month, I was waiting to see what happened. It was emotionally tormenting. Seven years passed and to my surprise, a baby was finally on its way. Joy and overwhelming happiness filled my home. The best 10 weeks of my life were spent dreaming of a nursery, a name, and whether the baby would be a boy or a girl. These thoughts kept me excited and smiling all the time. I was experiencing the perfect pregnancy glow. I couldn't imagine that soon after, sorrow would come knocking at my door when signs of a miscarriage threatened my pregnancy. I called my doctor only to hear him say, "Come to the emergency room." As my husband and I walked through that long cold hallway, my body trembled and tears of sadness were running down my cheeks at the thought of losing my baby. There was a blood test and then an ultrasound, which revealed I had an ectopic pregnancy and had to go into emergency surgery right away. That was a very dark and trying season in my life. Comments from family and friends abounded: "You'll be okay. You are healthy. It was only 10 weeks. You can get pregnant again." They tried to uplift my spirits, but no one could understand my pain. Many tears, many sleepless nights, many lonely days filled that season of my life. But like you've often heard, there is light at the end of the tunnel, and my light came in a form of a blessing.

I've had five pregnancies altogether: two miscarriages and in the end three amazing children have become a part of my story. Melody, Jason, and Melanie are my blessing and make up my beautiful family. They are my light at the end of the tunnel and my gift from God. As I look back at my journey, my life has been like labor pains. I don't remember the pain, but I certainly remember the joy. There! I allowed you into a very personal and private season of my life, hoping and praying that you realize you are not alone. Although my reality will be different from yours, one thing unites us. We both have a desire to put our family first, to give our children the very best of ourselves, and to help them become the best version of themselves.

At times, you will feel that no one understands your situation or your "why." You are convinced that you want to homeschool, but you don't have the slightest idea how to start. That was my situation at one point. I have good news: I am here to help! The guides and how-tos that I write about in this book are not fictional or invented theories; they are proven to work by my family. They are not other people's successes; they are my successes, and they can be yours, too. Although no two homeschool families are alike, you can use this book to ground yourself in the right direction when you find yourself lost or unsure.

Let me help you look beyond your limitations and toward your own successes with homeschooling. I believe you will be able to sit on your back porch 12 years from now and look back at the best decision you've ever made because of this book.

Unit 1

HOMESCHOOL AS A LIFESTYLE

After I decided to homeschool my children, I had to start making some changes to my lifestyle. What did homeschooling my children really mean? Was it something to do for a couple of hours of the day? Did it mean setting aside a specific time to teach math, reading, arithmetic, spelling, and science? All of those questions ran through my mind and I had no answers. I had no idea where to start or how to make it work. If you've ever had similar thoughts, I can assure you that I sense your frustration and sympathize with your confusion.

After resigning from my job as a schoolteacher, I knew I was going to commit fully to being a homeschool mom. I understood what I had to do with my children academically, but I was not certain how it would affect the rest of our lifestyle. So I decided to take in account what lifestyle changes needed to take place in order to make it all work. I read books and attended some seminars, but altogether they seemed a little antiquated and did not meet the needs or expectations I had for my family. At this time, I had a five-year-old and a newborn. I knew what I did not want, but I wasn't sure of what I wanted. Therefore, I decided to pick bits and pieces of what I had learned along the way and formulate my own lifestyle, something that would be manageable for our family. Some years earlier, in quest of an answer, I read an amazing book by Stephen R. Covey, *The 7 Habits of Highly Effective Families*. Among other things, Covey explains the importance of developing a family mission statement. This is exactly what my husband and I did. We jotted down what was important for our family, and from there we designed a lifestyle that was appropriate for us. It looked something like this:

> In our family, we will love unconditionally, respect one another, and teach our children the love of God. His Ten Commandments will be our moral code. Mission and service will be a priority and in keeping with this priority, we will teach our children the importance of developing a personal relationship with Jesus and the importance of living a healthy, modest life. Grandparents and extended family are very important, so we will stay close with them. We will take family vacations yearly. We value education, including higher education, and will work with our children to achieve their highest potential. The home will carry an atmosphere of peace. We will have open communication and

will let the children know what is expected of them. Dad will be the primary sustainer of our home and mom's priority will be homeschooling and raising the family. We will not forget to have fun as we go about our day. We will end the day with family time and worship.

With our mission statement clarified, my husband and I had a clearer vision of the family structure and we were both on board. This made it easy for us to have a guide for our new family lifestyle. Our home now had the right atmosphere. Our day would be guided by what we wrote in our family mission statement.

So our day went something like this: Our children would wake up to a peaceful atmosphere, music, and soft, kind words. As the children woke up, they were expected to nurture their relationship with Jesus and their love for one another. Mutual respect, even when family members are not in agreement, is to be present at all times. Health is very important to us. Therefore, healthy menus, daily exercise, and 10 hours of sleep every night are expected. As a mom, I was to display a sense of modesty that my daughters could imitate and follow. As a family, we sought to find any opportunity during the day to display mission and service towards others. The children needed to give their very best to learning. Education took place all day long, which meant seizing opportunities for teachable moments throughout the day instead of confining the learning process to a set number of hours. At the end of each day, time was made for the children to talk, explain situations, and share their points of view as we wrapped up the day with family time.

It seemed like a lot of work at first. And you may be asking yourself, "How am I going to do this?" It took some time, planning, and thinking, but once implemented, it was easy to follow. A family mission statement is something we still honor today and do not break. What is important to your family? How do you see your daily life and lifestyle? Don't be afraid. Change is always hard and sometimes will not be accepted by those around you. Don't let others determine your family's success or lifestyle. Envision what *can be*. Dream of the possibilities of a happy and healthy family and build your lifestyle around it.

Setting Up Space in the House

You probably wonder where you are going to set up space in the house for homeschooling. Do you need a room? Do you need a desk? Does the state require a specific class-like setting? I considered all of those questions, too. And the truth is that you already have toys, board games, Legos, trucks, and baby dolls everywhere. How are you expected to find room for a classroom, too? It can be an overwhelming thing to consider because you want to get it right. I remember going through the house trying to find the perfect spot for the kids' school. I thought about the kitchen, but there is too much going on there and I feared they won't be able to concentrate. I then thought about their room, but I realized I didn't want them to be secluded and without interaction for so many hours and their room should be a place for rest and relaxation. Turning the garage into a classroom was another option, but where would I put all my storage plus their bikes, exercise equipment, and treadmill. Ultimately, I decided that the playroom would be the perfect place for a school setting. We bought a desk, a chair, a chalkboard, a TV, a DVD player, shelves, and a corkboard. I decorated the room with posters on the walls, schedules, a reading area, a welcome sign, an American flag, and filled the drawers with pencils, pens, markers, chalk, construction paper, manipulatives, curriculum books, and notebooks. I was determined to make this room look just like a school. You may ask yourself whether all this is necessary. As a first-time homeschooling mom, you might feel that all of these things are because it is what you know. Your only point of reference is the time when you went to school and how it looked for you. Indeed, you might fear that if you gave your child any less or any different, things might not work out, as if the structure determines your child's success as a student or your success an educator.

The first day of school came and we were excited to introduce our daughter to her classroom. She seemed to enjoy it at first. Everything was new and neatly organized, so it gave her a sense of having her own space. After the first week, I saw her pick up her book and come to the dining room table close to the kitchen, where I spend most of my day. I asked her if she did not like the homeschool room and she replied, "I do, but I like it here better! I am closer to you." Since then, my kids have done school in the living room, at the dining room table, kitchen counter, bedroom, garage studio, family room, outdoors, and in the minivan. We still have the homeschool room as a place of reference, where all their schoolbooks and materials belong, but my children are free to do school where they feel most comfortable. Isn't that the point? To break away from the structure that limits them? To give them the freedom to learn in an open, comfortable space where they can create the environment in which they feel most comfortable?

Don't stress about finding the perfect place in the home to homeschool. Your children will find it on their own. It is more important to create a home base than a home space.

Your home is a school and when people walk into your home, they need to know that they've just entered a different zone. The atmosphere speaks homeschool. My children's assignments are displayed, their art is adorning our walls, their projects take center stage on our coffee tables and dining room table. In this way, when friends and family members visit us, our children's work can be acknowledged and they can feel proud of their work and accomplishments. Social media is another great way in which you can show their work and accomplishments to people you know or may not know. Your children will feel proud and you will be proud. Graduations, science or art fairs with the homeschool co-op group, recitals, sports games, talent shows, and plays are other great ways to invite friends and family to join in the homeschool experience. Our children always feel proud to share their accomplishments, which are a part of their homeschool life. Creating these types of settings and activities are an eye-opener for others into our homeschool world and community of homeschoolers, and a perfect way to have people over the house to see how homeschoolers really learn. Don't be afraid to show off your children's accomplishments and create a space for them; if you don't as a parent, who will? Our children need positive reinforcement, so it is our job to make them feel proud. It works; you'll see it on their faces and in their academic performance.

Applying these concepts is how the homeschool space is created, not by a four-walled classroom and not by replicating a school in your own home. Allow your children to learn where they feel learning can take place, and create an atmosphere where learning is what they do.

Homeschool with the End in Mind

This concept might be a little strange to wrap your head around at first. How can you have the end in mind? What end? Think of your child for a moment. Where do you see them at the end of this year? At the end of elementary school? At the end of high school? At the end of college? Visualize the end and work backward. My children were still small when some friends invited us to go on a Christian cruise vacation with them. My husband and I were excited because we had never taken part in one of these vacations and were looking forward to spending time alone without the kids. When we arrived, I was completely in shock to see so many Christian artists walking around and talking with guests. It was an amazing experience to be with so many authors of books I had read. That evening, we got a newspaper that detailed the activities and itinerary for the next day at sea. As I was browsing through it, deciding where I wanted to go or what I wanted to do, I saw a seminar by Lisa Whelchel that captured my attention. It was about homeschooling. I immediately signed up for it and can honestly tell you I could hardly sleep the night before from all the excitement. The next morning after breakfast, I went to her seminar on homeschooling and child-rearing and it was absolutely amazing. She introduced her family. Her children were exceptionally polite, kind, and well mannered. That night, my husband and I attended a concert and as I looked around, I saw Lisa with her children in the front row. As the music started, I saw her teenage kids stand up to praise and lift their hands in complete reverence to their Creator. I remember telling myself I don't want Christian children; I want spiritual children.

My goal from then on was to create an atmosphere where my children would have every opportunity to experience spirituality, such that I could see them navigating through life as spiritual people connected to God. As I started formulating where I wanted to end up, I realized that I needed to work backward and be intentional so that I could reach that goal. I saw I needed to put them in the right place with the right environment and the right possibilities for success. Sure, your children are going to have their own likes and dislikes, but if you know what outcome you want you can guide them in the right direction.

Children should be well rounded physically, spiritually, socially, and academically. There is much to consider here. For example, when defining pathways for social development or social interaction, it is important to consider what social skills you want your children to possess. When focusing on their academic development, you must ask yourself what kind of academic opportunities you intend to provide. This might include the right curriculum, co-op groups, or scholastic internships, just to name a few. How about their physical needs? Are sports, exercise, outdoor activities, and athletics what you consider most important? In all of these areas, what outcomes do you want to achieve? Design your plan and work on it with the end in mind, achieving your goal one step at a time. It is important to remember that this concept of working with the end in mind is a process. It includes vision, planning, and mission.

Vision

Vision, as stated in the *Collins Dictionary*, is the ability or an instance of great perception, especially of future development. Where do you see your family? Having a clear structure of what vision is allows you to have a clear direction towards your goal. Strategizing and planning for the future will give you the ability to work towards a plan that will help you rise above your current situation.

Vision is what an architect needs if they are to finish a project. An interior decorator has a vision for the project and looks beyond its imperfections. It is amusing for me to watch the television show *Fixer Upper* and see how Joanna and Chip Gaines can turn around the ugliest and worst house in the neighborhood and make it the most valuable. Vision is the drive that brings purpose to action and propels you towards something better. Imagine if you were going on a family vacation and had no destination. Vision takes you to that destination. When applied to your family, it can raise you above where you are, above what you've been taught, and above what you've been told. How, then, do you get that vision for your family? Give yourself some time. Examine where you are and where you want to be. If you come from a good home, consider areas you would like to improve. How would you like to make it different for your family? If you come from a home with a lot of baggage or you've made lots of mistakes along the way, then stop and consider what it would be like if you were able to change your destination. What is your goal? Once it is clear in your mind, blueprint it. Make a plan and stick by that plan. Two of the ways in which I have been able to make this happen in my own life are by having a vision board and by making a family mission statement. The vision board gives you a way to envision the future, and the mission statement gives you a rule book for your family. Yes, things change and get revised along the way as the children get older, but the roots have been planted deep. In this way, even if situations change, the goal remains the same. Now that we have laid the groundwork of vision, it's time to plan.

Plan

First comes the idea, then comes the vision, and now you are ready to plan! Think of yourself as a business owner considering what you want from your investment. Give yourself time and space to gather information, pray, and formulate a plan. As I pointed out, a vision board will allow you to see past today, past tomorrow, and take action. Be true to yourself. Write down 5 to 10, or even 20 things that you want your family to accomplish by the end of the year. Don't sell yourself short but be realistic. Take into consideration your children's age, gender, likes, and dislikes. Take your children's ideas and allow them to be a part of the process. Here are some examples: a family vacation, a garden, homeschooling, family time, spending time with grandparents, going on a mission trip, helping out in the community, music lessons, joining a co-op group, attending church. And after you have a clear mental picture of your starting point and your end point, it is time to lay out your plan. Remember to leave room for growing, making mistakes, structuring, and restructuring as you develop your plan. Make it fun! Announce the date and time when these family activities will take place and execute your plan.

Mission Board

Creating a mission board gives you the ability to visualize the whole picture. This mission board is derived from your family's mission statement. On your family vision board, make sure to set the goals you want your family to achieve as a whole for a given period of time. Set it up in such a way that each person contributes to how the goal can be achieved. Display the vision board in a place in the home where it can be visible for the whole family. Mission and vision work together as a team. Mission gives you purpose while vision is your navigation system. In this project, the entire family works towards one goal, which brings us to another phase of the homeschooling process.

Priority and Commitment

I had been married for over seven years before we had our first child. Our priorities consisted of ourselves, music, work, church, friends, extended family, and traveling. I had finished my bachelor's degree, as had my husband. We were very committed to our careers at that time in our lives. But suddenly, we were faced with a new responsibility, a family. We prayed for a family and God had answered our prayers. I knew that we had to make changes in order to ensure it would work. The focus was no longer ME, but WE. Our priorities had shifted to raising a family. We needed to be committed to this new lifestyle and the changes it demanded of us. It didn't mean that we had to give up everything forever. Some of the changes were for only a season in our lives and we all know that seasons come and go. But what you do for your children is ultimately lifelong and irreplaceable. I was committed to making them a priority. We implemented changes and not long after, we had a schedule and a routine to follow. Creating a homeschool structure gave me the grounds for putting my children and their homeschooling first. What followed was rearranging the day in a way that could work for all of us.

If homeschooling is your priority, then you are going to have to buckle up, rise to the challenge, commit to it, and make it happen. But why is that sometimes so hard to do? Most parents want it to happen, but when confronted with changing their lifestyle and giving up some of their ME time and flexibility, the demand can seem quite enormous. Some parents try to fit the homeschool lifestyle into their already-set lifestyle and it doesn't work. Homeschooling and its lifestyle get subordinated and that's why you meet a lot of discouraged parents, many of whom say, "I tried it and it didn't work" or "It's not for me." What are you willing to do to get what you want? Unfortunately, there is no easy way out. Creating a homeschool structure requires priority and commitment.

Put Your Children First

By creating a homeschool structure, you put your children first. We will look into planning your day using different schedules later in the book. Those schedules that a lot of us fear will give you a better understanding of how you can make time for everything you need to accomplish during the day. But, for now, we are talking about setting priorities and the number one priority for a successful homeschool is your child. There are many things that compete for our time. Up to now, life has been about YOU, but your lifestyle has taken a turn and you must re-prioritize.

To do so, you must have a clear understanding of the most important goal in your life and make the necessary adjustments to reach it. Assuming that we established earlier that your child and their homeschool is the priority, we must work to make this happen. Going back to your family mission statement, what is the single most important thing for your child's life? For me, it was spirituality. Any competing priority must take second place. Only by establishing your order of priorities will you have success in your homeschool. Set your priorities straight by putting your children first, restructure your life according to those priorities, and don't allow your day to be run by circumstances.

In our family, morning routines are important. Waking up, personal chores, time with God, and eating a healthy breakfast are part of a successful day. After morning routines, the priority is setting aside a good amount of time for schoolwork. Not only going through the subjects and getting good grades but learning the material. Core subjects have to be done daily and mastered in order to build a solid foundation. Music and musical instruments are very important and are included every day as a part of the schoolwork. Our children are very skilled in piano, violin, cello, bass guitar, guitar, and ukulele. Daily meals together as a family are also important in our home. They give us time to sit, talk, laugh, and sometimes even watch a TV show (most of the time *The Andy Griffith Show*) from which we can learn valuable lessons. This meal time allows us to discuss daily or current events, catch up with each other's interests, and open our hearts to one another. Exercise is also a priority. In order for us to maintain a healthy body, physical exercise needs to be done daily. Being at home, you are very limited by the amount of movement you get. That is why 30 to 45 minutes of exercise outdoors is a daily priority. However, in our family it does not take the place of extracurricular sports. Our children use this time to engage in doing an exercise video, play basketball outside, roller skate, skateboard, jog, and stretch. This outdoor time also gives an opportunity for getting sun and fresh air. When our son got older, weight training and going to the gym became other options.

Another unbreakable priority is family time. Right before bedtime, we huddle in our bed and have family time. This consists of bedtime stories, games, talks, and spiritual applications. Our kids know and look forward to this time nightly. Some of the best character-building discussions have taken place during this time. It has also been a time when family issues have been addressed and resolved. When our children were teenagers, my husband started to travel Monday through Friday for business. The change in his schedule required us to prioritize this time in a different way without omitting our tradition. FaceTime and Zoom calls with him each night became the new normal for us. Even when he was at work late or out for pleasure (Cubs games), he would excuse himself for a few minutes and join in the family time.

This is the level of priority and commitment I am talking about—the kind that tells your children THEY are first no matter what. The kind that does not break when circumstances change or when situations arise. Reevaluate your priorities and commitments to serve the homeschool lifestyle and your children. Make a plan that works for you and that you can follow—a plan that tells your children they come first!

Family Calendar

Because our schedules can get so compact, we are faced at times with having to rearrange activities and commitments because of unexpected situations. There are so many unexpected situations that can alter your day and take it in the wrong direction. Sometimes people have a perception that because you are home, you have all the time in the world and therefore it's fine to interrupt your day. We will talk about how to set boundaries at a later time. As I began to explore different ideas so that situations like these would not recur, I thought that working together on a family calendar would be important. We all became a part of scheduling the calendar, which started by writing down important information and appointments. First came important dates for the children. These included parties, playdates, tournaments, field trips, rehearsals, and recitals. Then we would go over our other important dates for the month, like medical appointments, weddings, meetings, choir rehearsals, late workdays, and date nights. Afterwards, we would see which days were still available, and then we would fill them in by visiting with grandparents, family, friends, and having visitors over the house. You name it, we would discuss it and write it down. This idea gave us a guide and freed us from unexpected changes in our daily and weekly routines. The children were aware of what was going on and did not feel that their priorities were being set aside. What we say we are going to do needs to be what we do! Any changes during the week or weekend, they are already aware of and prepared for. At times when the week held extra commitments and activities, our kids doubled up on assignments and put in extra practice during the afternoon in order to make time. Sharing from personal experience, creating a calendar can be very overwhelming, and you might feel that it is way too structured for the lifestyle you are used to living. Don't be discouraged! Scheduling will only make your life easier, by giving you a way to ensure your activities don't overlap or impinge upon each other. Put the finished calendar in a visible place. We kept ours on the refrigerator door and another one in the homeschool room as reminders. As the kids got older, they had calendars on their phones with alerts for upcoming events. Come up with a way that will keep your family organized and informed. When you find a system that works for the whole family, your lifestyle becomes doable, less stressful, and easy to manage.

Planning Makes Things Better

In my life, I have discovered that I need to plan ahead to make things better. As you already know, being organized is a key component to a successful homeschool lifestyle. With that said, it is not always easy. In order to make things work, lots of changes have to take place. But first things first. What kind of planning are we talking about? This time, we will talk about the kind of planning that will make this new lifestyle easy and successful so that you can optimize the highest potential of your family. The ultimate goal is for your day to run in a way that's organized and smooth.

As a new homeschool mom, I wanted things to run perfectly but that was not always the case. Kids would wake up at different times, meals took a long time to prepare, and at times I had to run out and buy groceries because I had run out of milk or other essential goods. The house was a mess. Laundry piled up for days and at times there was chaos everywhere. Occasionally, I found myself listening to podcasts on organization, wondering how these moms could hold it all together. I remember many times sitting in my bedroom asking myself if this job was more than I could handle. I prayed for my husband to come home early and give me a break.

Having a middle schooler, an elementary schooler, and a toddler was one of the most difficult experiences of my life. I was falling apart. I knew change had to come because there was no way to continue as I had. That's when I started to get inspiration from books, other moms, podcasts, seminars, and anything else I could get my hands on. I was looking to restructure my life because I felt like I could never get ahead and life was running me. No one system was perfect, but by this time I was willing to try anything! I started to implement a way that changed my outlook and gave me my life back. PLANNING! I had to plan ahead to make things better. So, I wrote down all the situations that were shifting my day-to-day in the wrong direction. For example: wake-up time, laundry, orderly home, meals, groceries, lesson plans, shopping, phone calls, texting, naps, dishes, bedtime. I decided to plan for them, not just write them on paper, but to have an action plan designed for when and how things were going to take place and get done.

Once I had this plan working, I gave it a test run until it was customized to fit my needs and the needs of my family. Where do you start? You start with you! What are the things that are not flowing, not taking place, or giving rise to chaos and stress in your life? I had my list, so I formulated a plan. If my planning was to be successful, I needed to prepare a day in advance. But the real planning for me started on Sunday. Every Sunday, I needed ME time to be able to plan for my week and organize it in a way that was manageable. Menus were made, I took time to look over my children's schoolwork and curriculum for that week, and paid close attention to the calendar events for Monday through Friday. After writing down what needed to take place in order to have a good and productive week, I formulated a plan to make it work. Kids go to bed every night by 10 PM. That way they are not up too early, and I have time in the morning for quiet time. I would get up by 6:30 AM, which gave me an hour and a half alone. This was my time to renew my strength, spend time with God, read, dream, journal, listen to a podcast, pray, go through my appointment book, and organize myself. At 8 AM, the kids wake up and the day begins. (When the kids got older, they got up a little earlier but the schedule for me stayed the same.)

Meals were planned out from Monday to Friday. Mondays involved grocery shopping with a daily menu to make meal preparations easier. Tuesday mornings, the children normally packed the minivan with what we needed for our day out (schoolwork, snacks, books, toys, games). Since it was a hectic day, we celebrated by calling it Taco Tuesday. Wednesdays was a perfect time to tidy up all the loose ends in the house. Drawers, closets, and kitchen cabinets got straightened, and front and back porches were swept and mopped. On Thursdays, bathrooms got cleaned, floors were mopped, and furniture was dusted. Fridays, the children attended Saints, our co-op group, and I had much-needed adult time with other moms. When the kids got older, we changed co-op to Thursdays and I swapped the days' activities. In the evenings, I got caught up on answering texts, returning or making phone calls, appointments, talking with friends, catching up with family, and so forth while the kids played sports. I cannot stress enough what a difference this planning made in my life and in the lives of those around me. I was not lost anymore. I had time for all the important things, which meant I wasn't falling behind. As the children got older, they were able to help more around the house and this is a true blessing. If your budget allows it, finding someone to do the heavy cleaning for you is an enormous blessing. I truly recommend it! Another way to take some weight off your back and free up some of your time might be to consider ordering your groceries online. This advancement in technology has certainly made my life easier and has given me extra hours to do more of what I want, like writing this book.

Creating a Family Dynamic with Your Spouse, Children, and Extended Family Members

Creating a Family Dynamic with Your Spouse

Creating a family dynamic where everyone is on board and feels valued is extremely difficult. Each family system is unique because we are all different. You are the only one who really knows what your family needs. With that said, patterns of relating and interacting with one another can become difficult in any family because every person is made unique. A healthy homeschool lifestyle requires that these patterns be identified, and that everyone's needs be met. Though we'd been married seven years before starting a family, both my husband and I lived lives in which we were very much independent people. We both had careers, personal bills, joint and separate bank accounts, nice cars, friends, and social circles. I remember being a newlywed couple and arriving at our first little apartment on a Sunday afternoon full with our luggage after our honeymoon. I asked my husband if he could set the luggage in the bedroom for me as I immediately started unpacking. I was alone in the room and minutes went by. I asked myself where my husband could possibly be. Our apartment was very small, so I knew he couldn't be far. I looked in the living room and there he was on our new white couch listening to Mariah Carey on his earphones. A flood of emotions overtook me, and I literally started to sob. As he looked at me, he could not understand what was going on. I know it sounds dramatic but I was in disbelief at the sight. First of all, he was sitting with his feet up on our new white couch, so I felt as if he didn't care about our furniture. Second, he was listening to music while I was putting all of our stuff back by myself. As a new wife, I imagined coming into our new apartment and unpacking together. After unpacking, I wanted us to sit on the floor (not to dirty our new white couch) and plan our first week together as a newlywed couple ready to face the world.

What was the problem here? Our expectations of each other were completely different. And this is exactly what happens when we operate independently of one another. When the family unit starts to grow with children, we need to go from independent to interdependent. This concept can create anxiety and stress. The increasing responsibilities, obligations, and expectations are overwhelming, and you do not have an instruction manual. This situation can make the family stronger or it can tear you apart.

I remember sitting in our favorite sushi restaurant, having a very intense conversation with my husband and asking ourselves, "How are we going to go from this independent lifestyle to a totally interdependent lifestyle?" The thought of having one income and being financially dependent on another person terrified me. Nevertheless, I was convinced that it was necessary for our growing family. What was certain was that my husband and I were anchored by our belief that love is a commitment. Knowing that made it less difficult to navigate what lay ahead for us. Rather than working apart (independence), we were going to work together (interdependence) because we were committed to each other and to our growing family. We couldn't let it just come to chance and hope it would automatically happen. We had to work at it and do something to allow interdependency to take place.

First, this meant creating the right dynamics with my husband. The financial and emotional aspects of this dynamic played a big role. My husband was now solely responsible for the finances of the home. He was the provider and therefore he carried a big load on his shoulders. To make this transition easier, we decided to give ourselves some time to work and pay off as many debts as possible. We wanted to live within our means and debt free. We still had our house, one car payment, insurances, and utilities. We set priorities and agreed on what was important and what was not. Pressure and struggles over money issues were not going to be a breaking point in our lives, so we decided to do our finances together and budget accordingly since we need money in order to live. We decided that we would be faithful in our tithing and trust God to take care of the rest. Providing financially for the family is a top priority for my husband, so we made his career important in our lives.

What about the emotional side of things? Remember my newlywed story at the beginning? The emotional side of a relationship can be a difficult strain for many couples from the very beginning. We knew that some of our dynamics had to change, but that can of course come with a bit of a struggle at times. For example: It has been a long and hard day at work. You are tired and want to go into your own space. Perhaps you want to escape into your own head by reading, listening to music, playing a musical instrument, or maybe golfing and going somewhere that doesn't require you to think much. Does this sound familiar? This scenario was our struggle because neither of us knew how to transition from emotional independence to emotional interdependence after a long day at work. We were committed to each other and to this new lifestyle and we were committed to loving. But change is hard and changing this dynamic was no piece of cake. It took high levels of maturity and planning. We were both eagerly waiting to disconnect from the day's doing, but we had it all wrong! In reality, we were disconnected all day, and this was the time to connect and draw strength from one another.

This is what worked for us! When my husband got home, we would give him a few minutes to disconnect from work, have dinner, and then he and I would go to the back porch to communicate. We would remind each other about upcoming events, raise any issues that happened during the day, share about work and its challenges, and connect more broadly. This allowed us to go from an independent day to an interdependent day. I mentioned before that creating this dynamic is not easy. One example is that the kids will interrupt, demand, and compete for your attention. Give them clear instructions and set expectations about the duration of your time together. The clarity you provide will help them come to a place of understanding and obedience. This may take training, patience, and redirection but it will work. In time, they will not interrupt, call, complain, or get in the way. Children get most of their security, emotional stability, and behavioral models from the way they see their mother and father treat each other. It is of vital importance for them to see that we chose each other, that we love each other, and that we value each other enough to spend quality time together. This not only helps us as a couple but secures and strengthens the whole family. This daily "US time" works better for us than the popular date night couples do. We needed to be in touch daily, and leaving our kids with sitters or family members meant more planning and sometimes detoxifying of character when we got back. We tested a couple of ways in which we could have this US time, and the method I've described here was by far the best. We also attended marriage retreats once a year and were able to get away, just the two of us. Many couples have different ways to make regular alone time. For example, as I mentioned before, some have date night weekly and that has proven to be the best way for them to reconnect and be alone. Others go away for an entire weekend once a month. Only you can decide what works for you. My husband holds a different job now, which keeps him away from home Mondays through Fridays. Our need for alone time is still very much there, and our commitment to one another is our unwavering foundation. We have made a point of talking every day at 5:30 PM. That is our US time, where we transition from being independent people to an interdependent couple and parents of our family. I am happy to tell you that our dynamic has changed considerably from that first day in our apartment.

Creating a Family Dynamic with Your Children

Creating a dynamic with your children is often difficult. Your children are a unique gift from God and they come with their own personality, their own likes and dislikes, and their own way of viewing the world around them. Yes, you can shape their personality to a certain extent, but the reality is that they are unique. When you have one child, you can focus all of your energy on that one child, but when the family starts to grow and you need to split yourself amongst them, that's when the challenge really begins. Our love for them is so great that we allow guilt to settle in and we start to do what is called emotional parenting. Emotional parenting creates a dynamic where the child can change the family or parenting culture to get their way. Children can manipulate your emotions. For many years I felt that if I didn't do what they wanted, they were not going to like me. How crazy is that! This kind of thinking leads to unhealthy parenting and in the end neither party wins. This manipulation can occur at any age. Until you realize that parenting is not about being popular or being your child's best friend, the dynamic will not change and you will continue to parent ineffectively because you will have created a false sense of reality for your child and yourself. No wonder the Bible says it so clearly in the Fifth Commandment: "Honor your father and mother." Not *like* your father and mother, not *love* your father and mother, but HONOR them. Parenting takes high levels of maturity and persistence. I often made the mistake of allowing my children's expressions of dissatisfaction reflect the quality of my parenting skills. What I didn't see at the time was that children often base their happiness on their wants rather than their needs.

When my children were little, my husband and I agreed that electronics were not going to be a big part of their lives. Television was only used for educational videos, biographies, home movies, or selected movies during family time. *Little House on the Prairie*, *The Andy Griffith Show*, and *Highway to Heaven* were some of the shows they regularly watched and they were used for character building. After each show, we discussed what we learned. With that said, we weren't completely against TV. Rather, we felt we would introduce it as they grew older and would not allow it to interfere with or become their source of entertainment. Of course, this became an issue because most of their friends had electronic games and watched endless hours of TV. They were constantly asked if they watched certain television shows and if they played certain video games, and our children always answered no. One Saturday night as we were driving home from church, one of our girls asked about *Hannah Montana*. I asked her where she heard this name. She said her friends were talking and asked her if she watched the show. My daughter answered no and her friends giggled at her, making her feel antiquated and weird. I saw the pain in my daughter's eyes as she was telling me the story and I felt bad. I questioned if I was too strict with my decisions if my children wished they were like everyone else. My heart and my emotions took control of my good judgment. The next day, I went to Sears department store and bought my daughter the works! I bought the princess TV and DVD player. I also called the cable company and, for the first time in 12 years, we had cable television. No more tears, no more feeling guilty, no more wanting to be like everyone else. I was not going to be that parent. Our daughter could not believe it and my husband was in shock. No restrictions! I had given in. One night after our usual family time, we prayed, kissed the children good night, and went to bed. As I was trying to fall asleep, I heard a voice speak to my heart. I got up from bed to see what was going on and to my surprise, the TV in my daughter's room was on.

I asked her why the TV was on at that time and she said she was not sleepy. We talked about the situation, I reminded her of the rules, and as I turned it off I realized I had made a big mistake. I allowed what other people thought of me to shake me and it wasn't working. In only one week, her attitude and her likes were completely different. Her eyes had been opened to a fantasy world made up of TV drama. Twenty seconds of advertisements can impact behaviors and put images in the brains of our children that cannot be erased. So, the question was who was going to educate my children—today's culture or me? For one week, I allowed the culture to make an impact on my daughter's life that was going to take some time to detoxify. Most children spend an average of 20 hours a week in front of the television set. This experience taught me a tremendous lesson. Needless to say, the TV and DVD player were out of the room and donated, cable TV was disconnected, and the actual cable that connected the cable TV into the television set was cut with scissors, never to be used again in that room. My husband and I spoke to our daughter and explained how I allowed my blind love for her to take charge of my value system.

We gave her our explanations and backed them with research. We then made clear how and when electronics and the media were going to be used in our home, and we have lived our lives by those standards ever since. Even more importantly, we have seen the benefits. I left a small piece of the cable TV hanging from the wall in my daughter's room to remind me at all times to parent with mind and not with emotions. You will have challenges! You will question yourself, you will make mistakes, and you will reroute and rise.

The rule still stands today. We don't allow TV in the bedrooms and only allow our children to watch movies and shows that are beneficial for character building. An outstanding American philosopher and psychologist William James suggested that when you are attempting to bring change, you need to make your resolve deep, seize the first moment to act on that resolve, and allow no exceptions. With that in mind, how do you create a dynamic with your children where they can distinguish between a matter of principle and a matter of preference? Where they can distinguish between needs and wants, where satisfaction surfaces dissatisfaction, and where guilt and fear are not the motivators? This can only be created on a foundation of trust, bond, security, assurance, acceptance, and unconditional love. In my experience, this bond with my children was established by reaching the hearts of each of my children with personal one-on-one time. When your children are small, you get small issues and problems, but as they get older those issues and problems get bigger. In his books, *The 5 Love Languages of Children* and *The 5 Love Languages of Teenagers*, Gary Chapman takes you through a series of languages that speak to a child's or teen's heart. I use this concept and their personal enneagram as my guide for the personal and intentional time I spend with them.

Once you have established this one-on-one dynamic with your child, be intentional. This is your one chance to help your child develop a bond with you and make an impression on their heart. Because you are home all day with them, you might feel this is taking place, but it is often not the case. We have three children, so I intentionally decided to meet on a one-on-one basis once a week with each child. My husband, on the other hand, decided that he was going to do intentional one-on-one bonding with each of them daily. No matter how you do it, what's most important is implementing and keeping up with your commitment. If you don't, your child will lose trust in you and what you say.

While this process might seem awkward at first, remember the one-on-one time is not about you. It is about your child. This means being completely present, putting your own personal interest, needs, and outlooks aside, and allowing your child to express his or her interests, ideas, goals, likes, dislikes, opinions, and views without being judged. The benefits will emerge as the bonding becomes stronger. Another thing to consider is that ages have stages, so you might have to change the circumstances even though the concept of one-on-one time remains the same.

Once you've captured your child's heart and trust has been forged between you both, you can rest in knowing that you've created a grounded dynamic from which your child will not depart.

Because I like to work from a schedule and we live on a budget, my daughters never really spent much time at the mall. One day as we were driving to and from engagements, one of my daughters said, "Mom, do we ever go to the mall? Or is that a place we'd rather not go?" I laughed because I realized that the mall was not one of our pastimes. We did not visit often, but they were becoming young ladies and curiosity was killing them. A perfect example of age and stage, this was an opportunity to add the mall into our one-on-one bonding time. They got what they wanted, and I could use this time to teach them a variety of life lessons. My girls presented a problem and together we came up with the solution. Here are a few one-on-one bonding time ideas to get you started. We've tested a number of these ideas with our children and seen excellent results.

Build-A-Bear Workshop
Date night
Ice-cream date
Sports game
Mall
Walks
Basketball one-on-one
Park
Broadway show

Concert
Dolphins season tickets
Puppy store
Gym
Cooking
Baking
Nail salon
Sports shop
Gala night
Mom and daughter retreat
Singing with dad
Going for a drive
Playing house
Building Legos
Making puzzles
Playing babies and Barbies
Putting on makeup
Antiquing
Fishing
Crafts
Watching *Star Wars*
Watching *Sunday Night Football*
Coffee shop

When my children reached teenage years, my husband changed jobs and started to travel during the week. Our kids were older, and the one-on-one bonding time shifted among them. Dad called each of them daily and made sure he spent one-on-one time via FaceTime or simply talking on the phone. He also spent time with them individually on Sundays when he was home. As a family, we were very clear about the changes in his schedule and how we would work with them to uphold the one-on-one time that had become such an important mainstay for our family. A deep sense of trust had been built between my husband and the children. Each one of them understood the changes that were taking place and were fine with them because they felt secure. The strong foundation had been laid, so when the circumstances changed the principle remained the same.

Creating a Family Dynamic with Grandparents and Other Family Members

It was a Saturday night, and I was extremely tired. Although I was not a fan of leaving the kids overnight at anyone's house, the exhaustion was overwhelming. My husband looked at me and in desperation said, "If your parents offer to take care of the kids tonight, please don't tell them no." At that moment, I knew that he was as exhausted as me. Our son was only six weeks old and my parents lived relatively close to us. Having already been parents of an infant, we had a mutual understanding of how to take care of our children and manage some rest. For example, my husband took the weekend shift with the newborn so that I could recharge from my weeknight duties and I took on weekdays so that he could have enough rest and be ready for days of work. But this particular weekend, we were both exhausted. Sure enough, my parents were always offering, and this weekend was no different.

I heard my cell phone ring! It was my mom. She asked her usual questions about the kids and us. Then she asked the question that we had been waiting for, "Would you like me and your dad to take care of the children so you guys can rest?" I immediately looked at my husband, who was nodding his head up and down as I softly replied, "That would be wonderful, Mom. Thanks." I packed the baby bag with all the essentials needed for a newborn to spend his first night at his grandparents' house. My older daughter was also going with them, so I got her all packed up, too. I gave my mom and dad all the instructions needed. We took the small bassinet, the humidifier, the noise reduction machine, and everything else I could think of for my baby to have a perfect night's sleep. I reminded my parents that he woke up every three hours and talked my mom through a tutorial on how to warm up the milk using a bottle-warmer gadget I'd purchased. My mom patiently said, "I got this, Rebeca. Go home and have some rest." Sleep, sleep, sleep was the only thing we could think about; as soon as we got home, we went straight to bed. It must have been 9 PM when I remember looking at the clock excitedly telling myself, "I am going to have a good 10 hours of sleep tonight." It must have been about 2 AM when I heard the phone ring. Completely startled, I focused on the caller ID only to see "Dad." I answered, not knowing what to expect. My dad said, "Rebeca, something is wrong with the baby. I think his ear hurts, he has not stopped crying on and off since you guys left. Can you please come?" I sensed the desperation in my dad's voice and answered, "I'll be right there." My parents had forgotten what it was like to have a newborn in the house. They had forgotten that babies cry, fuss, have colic, throw up, make funny noises, and the list goes on. Although I had taken all the essentials for them to have a "good" night, sometimes good intentions don't turn out as we plan. Needless to say, our son was fine. He was just displaying newborn characteristics. My parents, full of good intentions, couldn't handle the job because it wasn't their job.

Having children is the greatest responsibility ever given to humans. They are a blessing, and they are ours. Grandparents and extended family members play a very important role in the emotional aspect of child-rearing, but they are not the responsible party. Then how do we create a dynamic from which we can all benefit? Just as you are new to your role, so they are new to theirs. Grandparents have a lot of experience; they've gone through this process before and you can benefit from their knowledge. At the same time, you might be surprised that grandparents are completely emotional when it comes to their grandchildren. They indulge, spoil, bend every rule, and these little creatures can manipulate them into almost anything. One afternoon, my brother and his family were visiting my parents. We were all talking outside by the pool when we noticed that our children (all were under five except my oldest) were very quiet. We went looking for them and to our surprise, they had gathered every sheet, blanket, and comforter they could find in my parents' house and built a huge tent, or cave as they called it, that covered the entire living room. My parents thought that was amazing and creative, not caring that they had moved all the furniture around to make it happen or dirtied their linens, old and new.

My mom spent hours washing and folding them for days to come. Grandparents laugh at their grandchildren's jokes, cook their favorite meals, let them eat as much candy as they want, and give them a little money when you are not watching. How amazing is that! As amazing as it sounds to the child, children need boundaries, and grandparents are not wired for it. The truth is that they are not supposed to be. But you can't let your guard down. Parents, grandparents, and family members must all be in sync to make the process of raising children work. Creating this dynamic is difficult but not impossible.

Grandparents and extended family members have their special place in your children's lives, and that's just it—a place. It can be a safe place, a nurturing place, but not an indulging place. Grandparents should come to terms with supporting your lead as the parents. From there, you can work towards the same goals for your children. Grandparents don't always have to agree with your decisions, but they have to respect your choices. Establishing this dynamic in the right perspective will lay the groundwork for a relationship that will bless the children instead of disrupting and confusing them.

ACTION STEPS

"It is in the home that the education of the child is to begin."
—*Ellen G. White*

Unit 2

CURRICULUM

A concern that most homeschooling families have is, "How do I choose the right curriculum for my child?" When embarking on this journey, we want to do it right. We want to make sure our children are learning and excelling in whatever subject matter they're studying. There is a stereotype that homeschooled children are geniuses. The truth of the matter is that while there might be geniuses among homeschoolers, a high percentage of homeschooled children are average learners. The question remains, where do you start with choosing the right curriculum for your child? Keep in mind that most curriculums are written with the intention to take your child from not knowing a subject to mastering a subject. In order to determine which curriculum would benefit your child most, it is important to understand their learning style. Children learn in different ways and it is important that you seek out the avenues that will capture your child's mind most effectively. Keep in mind that what works for one will not work for all. I have three children and they all learn differently. When I started teaching the oldest one, I saved all of her books and teacher's manuals with the thinking that I could use them again with the other children. Ready and excited, I pulled out the old curriculum to teach my second child and, to my surprise, his interest, enthusiasm, and the light bulb moments I'd seen with my eldest were not there. Learning was increasingly boring for him. While my older daughter could sit and visually learn for hours, my son was active, hands-on, and auditory. My job was to meet his learning style. It is possible to go through school memorizing material without really getting an education and I did not want that. Homeschooling gives you the opportunity and the freedom to choose right.

While my children were in elementary and middle school, I did all the teaching myself. I found that there were many online and offline curriculums available, but I had a set of guidelines that I wanted to establish first. For example, when the children were little, I wanted them to do a lot of learning through play. Their playroom consisted primarily of educational and age-appropriate toys. I would rotate the toys as I saw my children master different tasks and stages. In our playroom, they had centers that would expose them to different kinds of learning styles and at an early age, I was able to distinguish which learning style appealed most to them. The children were also exposed to lots of sun, fresh air, and outdoor play to get their large motor skills developed. Learning through play is essential during those first years of life. Then it was time to start elementary school. An important principle at that stage was that our children needed to have a strong academic foundation. In the beginning, I stayed away from the structure of grade levels because I felt that the concept would box them in time-wise. If that happened, my children would be pressured by a beginning and an end. Instead, I was more interested in the quality of learning.

Having established this principle and the learning styles of my children, I went on to pick a curriculum. I wanted my children to have a strong foundation, and I was confident that mastering the basics would build the necessary foundation for successful higher learning. The foundational or core subjects I focused on included math, phonics, spelling, English, reading, and penmanship. They were nonnegotiable subjects during the elementary years and were done every day except Fridays. Everything else, such as history, science, music, and art, were done twice a week and with these subjects there was room for negotiation.

When people would ask what grade my children were in, I would often say, "Well, that depends on the subject!" For documentation purposes, I would always get them evaluated according to their age and where they were supposed to be. Suffice it to say, my children always tested average or above average (that will be covered later in this chapter). However, for learning purposes my children would move on as they mastered the subject in question.

Another consideration when choosing the right curriculum is that it needs to work for you as well as your child. I like choosing curriculums that I can understand and enjoy as a parent. I also like teaching all subjects out of the same curriculum. Other families like to pick and choose from different curriculums and that's fine. With that said, I have found that one curriculum works best for me when teaching three children in three different grades with three different learning styles.

There are times when you might get frustrated while teaching. Your children will, too, not because they don't understand the material or because the subject matter is hard. It is simply because you don't understand what you're teaching them. Let's face it, you were likely in school a long time ago. This is totally understandable, so don't feel like you've failed. You will find that you are learning all over again that you, too, need to work through the lessons and might need supplemental help to refresh in that subject matter and teach. One option I have found helpful is to call the curriculum company and ask for more information on how to best teach that particular subject. Hiring a tutor is another excellent choice. Regardless of the strategy you adopt, I have great news for you! Your child will be fine! Your child will learn! You have not damaged him or her academically. These are mere bumps on the road to success.

In addition to what I already mentioned, another priority for me was choosing a curriculum that would teach my children how to work independently. The curriculum would need to have clear instructions and supply all the materials needed. Using these materials, my children could clearly follow a progression of lessons. The final and most important consideration for me was that it would need to be a Christian curriculum that taught my kids from a Christian perspective. In this way, I can have peace of mind about what was being taught.

My advice? Narrow it down to at least three different curriculums that meet your expectations and test them. A good way to decide might be by attending a homeschool convention and meeting different curriculum vendors. Most of the time, they are willing to sit with you and walk you through their many options. These conventions are a good way to see firsthand the latest curriculums, learning and teaching techniques, as well as their success rates. Things to consider might be whether you want to do all the teaching, and whether you are okay with virtual learning or DVD streaming. I decided that I wanted to do all my teaching while my children were in their elementary years. For middle school and high school, my children did a DVD program with actual teachers and tutors available via telephone calls and I administered all their testing. My two younger children have done online classes with our county for their high school education and it has worked fine. Your state might have a complete curriculum or a FLEX program, which allows you to pick classes free of charge. One of the reasons we went this route is because I wanted my children to start facing demands and healthy pressures from the outside world. They have done very well.

Another important aspect when choosing a curriculum is for it to include what I call essential tasks or life management skills. Some curriculums might refer to them as home economics. I value these skill highly because they give my children the foundations necessary for real-life events. So often you hear people say, "I wished they taught me those skills in school." It is important that my children learn management skills now, instead of later, by trial and error.

Life management class might cover skills such as:

- Money and stewardship
- Budgeting
- Opening a bank account
- Basic sewing
- Balancing a checkbook
- Household chores
- Car maintenance
- Mission/good deeds
- Work projects
- Handywork
- Meal prep and cooking
- How to take care of pets
- Laundry
- Babysitting
- Quinceanera project
- Marriage project
- Baby project
- Lawn maintenance

Although this list might seem like part and parcel of a daily homeschool lifestyle, including them is crucial for life management success. This is an opportunity to decide what you want to teach and consider whether the curriculum is providing it.

Another recommendation, once your children start their senior year, I highly encourage you to have them do the dual enrollment program and take at least one college class while still at home to prepare for the next phase in their lives.

Give yourself permission to pick and choose, change your mind, ask questions, and start again. Stay away from comparing your children's academic success with others. Learn the curriculum, provide them with the necessary tools, and watch them flourish.

The "Later" Approach

We live in a culture that often praises overachievement in early education. As soon as the child turns three, parents are asked if they have started preschool yet, what school they attend, and what kind of curriculum they use. There are a variety of infomercials advertising reading programs that will have your toddler reading in no time. At times, these messages might lead you to believe that your child is behind. I hate to admit it, but I was one of those parents. I took personal satisfaction in spending time teaching my older daughter the alphabet by the age of 18 months and phonics by two years of age. Melody was reading one- and two-vowel words by the age of three. She was no prodigy, but I was determined to show the world what I called success. It made me proud every time I could show off my child and what she knew. The grandparents were brimming with pride at the thought of what their granddaughter could do at such an early age. By the time our son came, I had made my decision to stay at home full-time and start homeschooling. I soon concluded, after reading, researching, and investigating, that although children are capable of reading, solving mathematical equations, playing instruments, and learning different languages at a very early age, it is not necessarily what is best for them. What's more, these early achievements aren't necessarily indicators of a high GPA in high school or a foot in a good university. Putting children in an early education program, sitting them at a desk for three to five hours a day, limiting their playing time, and constricting their life experiences can only result in depriving them of a true education.

Although our older daughter did very well in grade school, college, and later in pharmacy school, we decided that we would wait and take the approach of "better late than early" with our other children. We would not stress their little brains at an early age, but would instead wait for age-appropriate learning. Our son has always pushed himself because he is intrinsically motivated. He is very determined and a problem solver, so he started kindergarten and did not waste any time. He was always keeping pace with his age and grade. We purposely started our younger daughter later. She picked up and mastered reading at age eight and continued moving on at her own pace. In high school, she is very independent, a self-motivator, and an A student. She does all of this on her own, working at her own pace, and mastering every subject. Three different children, three different approaches.

Homeschooling gives you the freedom to accelerate or slow down when needed. More broadly, it gives parents the means to determine what is best for their children instead of putting them in an institution with no choices. So many children get labeled and pushed when they are simply not ready. Still other children are not stimulated and challenged enough; as a result, they end up being slowed down by a pace that is not their own. Who is going to pick the curriculum for your children? Who is going to determine how they learn? Today's culture or you?

The Importance of a Support Group

When my older daughter was about eight years of age, she came to me one night and asked me: "Mami, what is that place called school that all my friends talk about?" My heart sunk, realizing that she was curious about school. I sat her down and explained with clarity what school was about. She then asked me the dreadful question every homeschool mom wishes their child would never ask, "When am I going there?" I looked into her eyes and told her, "Melody, you are in school. You do school at home." "Why?" she asked. I knew then that I had to be completely forthright about our reasons for homeschooling her. She listened, looked straight at me, and said, "I love to homeschool, thanks." That was it! Children need to know the truth about your decisions so they can stand strong. Be clear and concise. You need to be able to reach their hearts in a truthful and loving way. If you are able to accomplish this they will understand and start enjoying the homeschool experience.

I remember when my children were 12, 6, and 3. As our older daughter was approaching her teenage years and our son, my middle child, had lots of energy, I knew that it was time to find a support group where some of their needs could be met. I wanted a place where our children could be themselves and be around like-minded friends, and where our son could play and exercise.

A friend told me about a support group that her children enjoyed, so I decided to give it a try. As I arrived that Friday afternoon, I was totally impressed. I can still remember the smiling and loving faces of the two kids who welcomed us at the entrance. The director of the group immediately came over to greet us and to meet my children. I felt like I had arrived at the right place. The children there were courteous, obedient, humble, spiritual, and their motto was "Lift each other up, never tear each other down." I knew I had found the right place for my kids. I wanted them to have positive experiences with other homeschool children and socialize with them. And they did. For four years we made this support group our family, and every Friday afternoon we would look forward to meeting our friends at the park. The kids would join in their activities and some of us moms would get together and walk the trail, plan for the upcoming week, read, talk, and exchange ideas. This group was not only good for my children, it was also wonderful for me. Don't be afraid to try; your children need an outlet and so do you.

During the summer of 2014, I came up with an idea. I had been praying to God to lead me in the right direction. Although we were very happy with our support group, I wanted to be able to share what I had learned and encourage other moms in their homeschooling experience. That is how I came to create my own homeschool support group. I partnered with other moms who had the same vision and desire, and we came up with a plan. We wanted our children to be God's light. We invited more moms to share in our vision and brought our proposal to our church board. They welcomed us with open arms. The support group met once a week on Thursdays at our church facilities. We had T-shirts, banners, invitations, as well as a prayer group for moms before the actual support group started. Our homeschool support group met from 11 AM to about 2:30 PM. This gave the children time for worship, theme lessons, lunch together, monthly field trips, and playtime. Our children had a place to celebrate birthdays, attend art fairs, reading fairs, science fairs, talent shows, and were able to show what they were learning to family and friends. Our support group also gave us a venue where we could have yearly graduation ceremonies, traveling experiences, camping, family picnics, and community service with complete parental involvement and a yearbook. And it was free! Each mom would take care of the teaching material for one month and then alternate. Looking back now, I know I would never have found the quality of dedication, selflessness, and commitment from these moms unless God handpicked them Himself and I am positive that He did. We named this support group His Light for a reason.

What is stopping you from finding the right support group? You don't have to carry the homeschooling load yourself. There are wonderful co-ops and support groups ready to give you a helping hand. Botanical gardens, museums, aquariums, and county fairs often offer classes for homeschoolers. There, your child can participate and learn hands-on with other children. All you have to do is place your child in the right environment for them. Or maybe you are just like me and have the desire to start your own homeschool support group, which can help you make a difference for your own children and others. If you are in a desperate situation because you don't know what to do or where to go but your children might need this support, I am here to help you get started and situated on the right path. Don't let fear or anxiety stop you. Finding the right support group for your children can make the difference for all of you. The right support group will give your children a place where they truly belong and where experiences and memories can be forged. The possibilities are endless, regardless of whether you create them or join one already created for you.

Extracurricular Activities

There was a season in our homeschool life when my children were busy with extracurricular activities. Piano lessons at 10 AM, violin lessons at 11:30 AM, ice-skating lessons at 12 PM, and lunch at 1:15 PM would comprise our Tuesdays.

The day continued with gymnastics at 2:00 PM, knitting club from 3:30–4 PM, guitar lessons from 4:15–5:15 PM, and baseball or basketball at 5:30 PM. Needless to say, Tuesdays were very long. But let me tell you, there were so many memories created as we drove all over town to get to these extracurricular activities. The schooling was done in the minivan, and our day took a variety of forms including singing, crafts, games, music, movies, and naps. The van was set up with two different DVD players. One was in the back seat for my oldest daughter to do school and the other was in the middle seat for my younger children. Once we got to our destination, I would sit in the middle seat and do schoolwork or answer questions on a given subject for the children who were not involved in the extracurricular activity at the time. During this time, their lessons would get reviewed, the curriculum would get explained, their assignments would get graded, and off we went to our next destination. Depending on whose turn it was to do the extracurricular activity, I would stay with the other two of my children and do the same. At lunchtime, we would find a place to eat tacos. Here, we'd pause and talk about their dreams, goals, likes and dislikes, and we would go around until everyone had a chance to share. We even had time to laugh and sometimes cry. Lots of memories were made on our Taco Tuesdays, as we called it.

Our other days were fun, too. Mondays were spent at home so we could start off the school week strong. Wednesdays were also a home-based day, and Friday mornings consisted of catching up if they were behind in a subject or make up if needed and getting ready for the Sabbath, our day of spiritual rest. On Fridays, school ended at 12 PM and afternoons were dedicated to chores, hobbies, and baking before going to our homeschool co-op.

Days can be long, but the years are short. Don't let my experiences overwhelm you. What I've shared with you is what worked for me, the secrets that I feel gave me success in my homeschooling journey. You know your family best and you know their needs. My children need stimulation to keep them focused and achieving. Some families might need less or might need a different pace. The secret is to be able to adjust to the needs of your children as you see fit. Seasons might come into your life where they are quiet and where you choose to take a sabbatical from everything around you to recharge and refocus. We've had those, too, and that is also part of our curriculum and lifestyle. We teach them that they need to know when it is time to go and when it's time to stop. There is not a cookie-cutter way of doing things, for as they grow you also grow. What you should know is where you want to end up. No one can say there is only one way. Don't let a system pick for your children or make them choose which electives to take or which extracurricular activities to engage in. *You* are the mastermind at designing what is beneficial for your family and how you want them to spend their extracurricular time. This is a great responsibility but it's also a great freedom. Dare to dream and design. Empower your children with guidance, planning, and approval.

Certified Curriculums and Umbrella Schools

While most curriculums give you the option of accredited or nonaccredited, all that really means is that you have the option to abide by their organization or not. Most of the time it is the same company you bought the curriculum from giving you the choice. Therefore, both are official. All the word "accredited" means is that they are giving you the option to keep records, administer testing, record school days, and will provide you with an official report card at the end of the school year as mandated by the state. No doubt, this is a great option for some families because it keeps them well organized and on task. In addition, your child is registered in their school system. Another option is choosing the nonaccredited curriculum, which means you would buy the curriculum and have complete control over it. In doing so, you'd need to register your child in a school system, whether that be in your county or at an umbrella school, and abide by their rules and regulations.

By the time your child turns six years of age, most states require that he or she should be registered. Children need education and the state requires it. In order for you to avoid investigations later on, it is best for you to register your child. Every county has a homeschool office and their requirements are simple. A letter of intent is your first step and that can easily be found online or through a visit to the homeschooling office. Regardless of what curriculum you choose, they will guide you capably and answer any questions about what your county expects. If you choose to go this route, the state gives you control over the curriculum of your choice and sometimes even offers a curriculum online completely free of charge. I know my state does. Another way in which you can administer your own curriculum and keep your own pace is by finding a good accredited umbrella school. I have used all three options mentioned here and I will give you my opinion on all of them.

First, the accredited option. I used this option when my children were in elementary school. New to homeschooling, I needed a place where everything was set out for me. The accredited option was great because they administered their own testing and kept me on track. I was able to register my child through their accredited option and have her registered in the school system. The curriculum company will give you an official report card at the end of the school year, which is beneficial to have. In short, the accredited option is a safe and structured way to complete a school year. With that said, it does not leave a lot of room for your children to work at their own pace. It will keep them on a time restraint from start to finish.

Then, there is the nonaccredited option, from which I believe my children benefitted most. This option gives you the choice to pick and choose curriculums, administer your own testing, work year-round, and gives your children the freedom to learn at their own pace. If you choose this style, you must have your children registered by your county. You may feel that this option is more complicated and sounds like a lot of work, but it seemed to work best for me. I registered my children with the county and in an umbrella school. The county requisites are very minimal and are not hard to obtain. They require a yearly evaluation of your child by a certified teacher, a portfolio of your child's work, and any state testing that your child has done, which in many cases is optional.

If your state offers an online curriculum, then the grade automatically gets recorded into the system without the need for any type of evaluation or portfolio. Another perk is that when your child enters high school, it is easier for them to opt for dual enrollment with the community college or state university that may be offering the program. You might then wonder why I also register my children with an umbrella school.

Umbrella schools give you, the parent and child, yet another option. For the parent, it gives peace of mind. For the child, it gives them a sense of belonging to an institution, which is very important. This is a good option when your child enters high school. With that said, many parents use umbrella schools throughout their children's schooling and it works out well for them. An umbrella school gives you the choice of curriculum, the freedom to work at your own pace, student involvement, and a physical structure your child can call school. Why do I use this method for high school? It's a matter of choice and priority. At the end of your child's senior year, they will have to take the GED and receive their diploma. As a parent, you must find a company that can produce an official high school transcript or do it yourself. I did not want my children to end this season in their lives in this way. As a result, I opted to enroll them in an umbrella school. An umbrella school is accredited by the state, which means it protects you and your child. It shadows you and gives your child an institution to which they belong, with a name, a diploma, and an official transcript. It also makes them accountable for graduation requirements such as SAT, ACT, and FAFSA applications. Lastly, it allows for scholarship opportunities. There are many umbrella schools throughout the country that are very reputable and have very high standards.

How to Make a Portfolio

While portfolios are not a requirement in all states as part of your child's yearly evaluation, they are a wonderful way to keep your child's work and their masterpieces in one place. There are companies that will create the portfolios for you, but overall it is pretty simple. I have included a list of what I have found to be most helpful:

Traditional Portfolio

- 3-inch portfolio
- File folders
- Three-hole punch
- Laminating clear sheets, tabs
- Cover page with the child's picture and grade
- Outline

- Legal and other important documents (copy of the letter of intent, copy of birth certificate)
- Curriculum used
- Learning objectives
- Work samples for all academic subjects by categories
- Book logs
- Read-aloud book log
- Individual student book log
- Gameschooling log (yes, games do count!)
- Extracurricular activities
- Clubs attended
- Musical instruments played and recital certificates
- Monthly schedule activity log
- Field trips
- Films and documentaries watched
- Live music and theater performances (praise and worship)
- Awards and certificates
- Community service hours
- Tickets, brochures, and other memorabilia from field trips, vacations, and adventures
- Artwork
- Photos of large projects
- Fitness log
- Pictures of performances
- Photos of everything

Digital or Online Portfolio

Another good option, if you are comfortable with technology, is a digital portfolio. They are a wonderful way to keep your records on your computer. There are many sites that offer blogging options such as Blogger, Weebly, and WordPress, just to mention a few. For more tech-savvy moms, these blogging options are a great way to create a digital homeschool portfolio and make it easy to share content with family and friends. They give you an alternative to going paperless and free up your home space. In addition, they are easy to submit to your evaluator online. You also have the option to get them printed, which can make for a wonderful keepsake. There are many options and companies but here are two of my favorites. They have proven with time that they are reliable. I have listed some reasons why you might want to give them a try.

Evernote is a great option for:

- List making
- Lesson planning
- Brain dump
- Saving ideas from the web
- Saving articles
- Scanning and saving documents
- Uploading photos

Seesaw is another wonderful digital choice. Here is why I like it:

- It is free
- It is designed for students to use
- It allows the student to showcase their work
- Very simple to use and you can upload the day's work in seconds and stay organized
- Good customer support
- Shares ideas for using the app
- Students can upload videos, audio recordings, drawings, links to the web, or PDFs
- Students can create and maintain their own blog

In addition to these options, your children can work on their own portfolio online. They can use their Instagram for pictures and documentation. There are also kid-friendly blogs that they can use to document their school progress. These features keep them excited and, all in all, they make for a fun way to take pride in their accomplishments at the end of a school year.

Evaluations, Testing, and Laws of Homeschooling

This is probably the most serious part of the book, but it is information that most families will want to know right away. What are the requirements for homeschooling? What evaluations and attendance records are needed? What type of testing is available? Are there any laws I need to know? What credentials do I need to be able to homeschool my child? Without a doubt, all of these questions can give rise to a lot of stress. I know I was stressed when navigating them. More specifically, I was very scared of getting it all wrong and being investigated by the government for not fulfilling the right requirements as a parent. The good news is that it is simpler than you think, more accessible than you imagine, and very affordable. While most states have a homeschooling office where you can get your state information and regulations for educating your child, it is often affiliated with the school board association. Although homeschooling has always existed in some form, it has become exceptionally popular in recent years. The number of homeschooling families has consistently grown in each state with each passing year. The coronavirus pandemic has made homeschooling very popular, and most families in our country in some form or another has had a taste of what homeschooling or home education is about. How fortunate are we that it is available! In the United States, the Supreme Court has ruled that parents have a fundamental right to direct the education of their children. Therefore, homeschooling is a right as long as the child is safe, treated with affection, educated, has medical care, and is protected against cruelty and abuse. Who can educate? That is up to you.

Evaluations, testing, attendance, and portfolios vary from state to state, so you should always be aware and check that you are in compliance. One thing is for certain: Parents do not need any teaching credentials or certifications to do the job. You are fully entrusted by the state and by God. What an amazing privilege! What an opportunity! What a responsibility! If I could do it all over again, I would do it without hesitation. It is the best decision we ever took as parents. So, what is stopping you?

For the most part, this all sounds manageable. But what do you do when graduation, college testing, SAT scores, transcripts, and scholarships start knocking at your door? I remember feeling lost and anxious when my firstborn entered high school. In elementary and middle school things kind of flow, but when your child enters high school everything changes and there are a series of things you must comply with if they intend to apply to college or university. I was at a loss, so I called a friend and expressed my desperation, "I think this is too much for me and I don't know what to do," I said. At that time, she was in the process of graduating her third child and her fourth was starting high school. God has always put the right people in my path to help when I have needed help. In this case, my friend gave me a very important piece of advice. She said, "Don't believe everything you hear and get your information from the right source. If you do so, you will be well informed and your child will be on the right track." Though her advice was simple, it made all the difference and so it is the advice I want to give you today. Go to the right source and get well informed. Every state is different and has different requirements for graduation, testing, and college or university applications. What is important is that you meet the requirements for the college or university your child wants to attend. Let me give you peace of mind and reassure you that you are doing the right thing and that you are on the right path.

Peace of mind #1:

Most states do not maintain guidelines for graduating a homeschooled student. In most cases, the homeschooling parent determines the graduation requirements for the student (your child). Upon completion of those requirements, you can issue your graduate a high school diploma.

Peace of mind #2

Homeschooled students may obtain a high school diploma in several ways. From parents, from an umbrella school, from a virtual school, from a correspondence school, from their accredited curriculum institution, or from a GED.

Peace of mind #3

Students who are homeschooled through an umbrella school or a correspondence school will receive a diploma and transcript from that institution (my favorite choice). Similarly, students who are educated through a virtual online charter school or online public school are also granted diplomas. Make sure you investigate the program before making a choice.

Peace of mind #4

Homeschoolers do not need a GED or a diploma to apply to college, to qualify for financial aid, or to take the SAT, ACT, or any other placement exam. They simply need to declare that their homeschool education meets state law requirements and that they have the credit requirements and a transcript.

Peace of mind #5

What all this means is that you can determine what type of graduation and diploma you want for your child. When your child enters high school or ninth grade, you can come up with a four-year plan for credit and class compliance to meet the requirement for their choice of college or university. Some parents choose to follow public-school requirements, thinking that this will give their children a better chance of getting into college, but it is not necessarily so. In the end, it is up to you. Colleges know that states have varying requirements. Therefore, their admission policies are not based on them. What you really need is an official homeschool transcript that will show your child's academic history.

Don't allow fear of the unknown to determine your child's college trajectory. It is often people who have no real foundations for their unsolicited advice who plant seeds of doubt. The schoolteacher, the family member, the private school principal, the neighbor—they will be your biggest critics. They are often people who have no clue about homeschooling, and yet voice their opinion with authority. Believe me, those are often the hardest people to convince. Don't accept unsolicited information and research your state homeschool laws. You don't have to have anything other than what your state requires or mandates. It is your choice from kindergarten to senior year.

Finding Your Children's Passion and Career Interest

Working with your child's future in mind gives you the opportunity to guide your children through the present. This concept is put into practice at every stage of the homeschool lifestyle. I do not recommend talking about career choices in their last year of high school or to begin taking stock of their interests when they are about to graduate. It takes time to prepare them for their future, but taking that time is a great blessing.

At times their career choices will seem outrageous but remember that you are giving them opportunities to discover and share their interests through the process of exploration. Your job as a homeschool parent is to listen and encourage them. As you already know, we have three children, and they are all very different. When our daughter Melody was young, we would visit the zoo very often. One Sunday afternoon, as we entered the zoo, she looked at us and said, "I know what I want to do when I grow up." My husband and I excitedly asked, "What?" as she answered, as proud as could be, "I want to pass out the maps at the zoo." At that moment, she thought she had found the best career ever! I breathed deeply and then replied, "And you would be the best at it!" Her dream was not crushed and she went on to have other dreams, like working at Subway, going to the Olympics and getting a gold medal for figure skating, working in the White House, and so on. Along the way, we continued to encourage and explore with her as she moved through different stages. Today she is pursuing her dream at Loma Linda University School of Pharmacy.

Our son, Jason, had dreams of becoming a baseball player and going to the major leagues. He really has talent. One day, on our way to a Little League championship game, he looked at his dad and with complete innocence and a sparkle in his eyes, he said, "Papi, my team is going to the World Series!" Was it really? No! But in his mind, he was going there. What was our job again? Because we encouraged and explored all the different possibilities with him, he went on to play basketball, win championships, and explore other sports. Another time he said to us on the way home from church, "I know what I want to be when I grow up!" He had already warned us about the major leagues, so we were expecting anything at this point. "I want to be a reader man like Pastor Freddy." He loved our youth pastor and his preaching and wanted to be just like him. Today our son has aspirations to become an attorney and we are supporting him in that endeavor. Seasons change, but when we encourage our children, we have the power to shift their mindset into the "I can" instead of the "I can't." We need to be able to convey to them that they are so important to us that what they want to do matters.

Our third child is a gem. She is always finding innovative ways in which she can put her talents to work and make money. Beginning at five years of age, she had her first business selling her old toys in the church parking lot. Later, she went on to make flyers for her dog-walking service and placed them all over our neighborhood. And every so often, she would come up with a new and creative business, like selling slimy slimes, bracelets, and even her own paintings. Being an entrepreneur is in her blood. She must have been seven years old when we traveled to Kennedy Space Center for the first time. On the way back, she excitedly said, "I know what I want to be when I grow up!" As with our two other children, we excitedly asked, "What?" She answered as if she'd just experienced a light bulb moment, "I am going to be an astronaut!" She said it with all the confidence in the world. You could feel her passion. Since then, she has aspired to own her own bakery, go to the Olympics and compete in gymnastics, star in a Broadway musical, work as a veterinarian, become a dermatologist, and she is still exploring possibilities. Don't crush your child's dreams and don't discourage their passions. Your job is to encourage them to explore all the possibilities and refine the process as they approach their goal.

So often we limit our children by imposing our thinking when in reality there are hundreds of career opportunities from which they could choose. We will always encourage our children in whatever field they finally decide to choose. However, we ask that they always keep four questions in mind: How can this career help me serve others? Will this career go hand in hand with my faith and value system? How can this career help me grow? How will this career affect my family?

Some people might have looked at what we were doing with our children and thought that we were encouraging a dream with no real future. But what we were really doing as parents was giving them the tools to have the firsthand experience and work through the solution. This includes allowing them to explore and giving them permission to change their minds. We are still encouraging and exploring with them, shaping and guiding them so they can discover where God wants them and needs them.

Shadowing and Volunteering

After my children showed interest and researched a particular career, I knew we were ready for the next phase, which we call shadowing. Our older daughter decided that she wanted to be a pharmacist very early on. She had many other interests, but she was passionate about that career above all else. I can pinpoint when it first began. We went to a memorial service for the son of a dear friend of ours. The young man had died of cancer. Before he passed, he studied and worked as a pharmacologist. At the memorial, they spoke about his life and accomplishments. That event impressed her mind and heart in such a way that she knew at that moment what she wanted to be and did not change her mind. Our son had a similar experience. People often asked him the typical question, "What do you want to be when you grow up?" He always had the same answer, "I don't know yet." As parents, we tried to give him as much exposure as possible, but he couldn't quite narrow his options. One day, we visited the county courthouse with our homeschool support group, His Light. The children were able to experience sitting in different courtrooms, listening to small court cases, and seeing firsthand what went on inside. They were even able to visit the jailhouse where the accused spent the night until bail was posted on their behalf. After one of the court cases, the judge welcomed our group and went on to say how she had been homeschooled by her mom and how happy she was to have us visit. This event again made such an impression on my son's heart and mind that he decided he wanted to become a lawyer. It is amazing how I believe God puts you in the right place to impress upon your children where He will use them the most. Do not get boxed in limiting thinking. Give your children the opportunity to wander and explore the possibilities. Our youngest, Melanie, is still exploring her talents and potentials.

What, then, is shadowing? After our children showed interest and maintained some consistency about their career of choice, we looked for a place where they could volunteer their time and learn about their career of choice. You will be amazed by how many companies welcome this idea. Memorial Hospital Miramar was one of them. Our daughter was able to shadow a pharmacist for a whole year and learn firsthand about the occupation. She gained knowledge, trust, and confidence in a field that started as a dream and later became her career of choice. In addition, she was acquiring community hours, a prerequisite for graduation and scholarships. They were even able to give her a recommendation letter when it was time to apply for pharmacy school. Our son, Jason, has gone through a similar process of shadowing. God connected us with a young attorney with an office in the heart of the city. When the time was right, I gave him a call and again the opportunity was there. Jason shadowed three days a week for four hours each day. During that time, he gained knowledge, respect, self-confidence, and was able to learn and be taught in an area unbeknownst to him. And now his decision stands strong to pursue law. It is a powerful resource to be able to give our children opportunities to explore and grow.

Unit 2: Curriculum

ACTION STEPS

"Homeschooling allows you the freedom to step off the highway of learning and take a more scenic route along a dirt road."
—Tamara L. Chilver

Unit 3

CHILDREN'S DAILY SCHEDULES AND ROUTINES

Keeping a peaceful home is important for our children and ourselves. An atmosphere of love and calm gives children the ability to concentrate. On the contrary, when there is turbulence and chaos, the children feel out of control and they can't concentrate and be effective. Things like soft music, essential oils, and kind and soft words set the tone for the day. As a mom, you need to be ready to talk to your children and address situations if they feel uneasy. Give them a break, pray with them, and start over. One of the ways in which I have been able to accomplish this is with the use of daily schedules. Some parents cringe at the thought of having to manage their lives with a schedule. What they don't realize is that their day can be so much more enjoyable this way. Without a schedule, even the sweetest of words like, "Mommy, what do I do now?" can turn into a stressful moment. Many parents are unsure how to start, so they follow a schedule that is not fit for them or their children's needs. This will bring failure and potentially reinforce the belief that "schedules do not work for me." Discipline and rules are hard. We are so used to doing our own thing and following our own path that introducing daily planning or a schedule can become painful because we feel limited. However, when seen from a different perspective, it could be the answer you have been seeking. Keep in mind everyone is different, every household has different needs, and every family has different dynamics. I recommend you make a personalized schedule, and I promise this will bring peace into your home. I find schedules extremely important because they give my family direction throughout the day. They point out what needs to be done and keep everyone on the right path. You might not get it right the first time, but you'll get there and it will be worth it. I will guide you through a set of schedules and show you how to build your own.

From infancy to preschool, it is very important that you keep a routine. This will give your child a foundation for schedules later on. Routines are a wonderful way to accustom the brain to following a pattern, and soon your child will start to follow it all on their own. I introduced a schedule after the routine had been working for a while.

When your child is between three and five years of age, I would suggest bringing out a simple picture schedule. You could print these out on Chart Jungle printables or make your own with customized pictures. A picture schedule is easy for young children to follow. Generally speaking, children at this age do well when they know what is expected of them. Therefore, I would suggest giving them clear and concise explanations of how the schedule works and what is expected of them. Be specific, and do not change or bend the rules. Leave room for error, as this is all new to them. The way I worked with my children is that every Sunday I posted a schedule for the school week in their bedroom or homeschool room. Every time they completed a task or chore, they received a happy face sticker on that square corresponding to it. I would check these at the end of each day, and if they did not do a task or had a problem completing a task/chore, they would be encouraged to do better the next day or be pointed to the fact that help might be needed. The happy face was not given in response to how well they did the task. Instead, it was given for completing it and trying. At the end of the week, they received a golden coin for each day completed. Accordingly, they could collect five golden coins by the end of the week, which was the equivalent of five dollars to spend as they wished. It wasn't payment, it was a reward!

The hardest stage of life for implementing a new task is when children are little. Everything is new to them. Concepts are not as easy to grasp and remember. This is the time to work really hard with them and instill patterns of behavior and obedience so a foundation is created for their lives. My children loved positive reinforcements and new challenges. For that reason, I tended to use a lot of positive reinforcements to train their thinking and behavior toward positivity. Once they correlated following a schedule with something positive, they were more likely to want to do it and to do it with a cheerful spirit. Be consistent!

From five to ten years of age, the schedule changes. Now children can read and are able to handle more responsibility. At this time, some form of schooling is also taking place. You have implemented a routine when your child was an infant, a picture schedule with rewards when they were a preschooler, and now it's time to transition to a full day's schedule. As a result of all the previous work you've done, the adjustment should not be so hard. Keep in mind that you are the one who knows your child the best. This means you know how to motivate them and ensure the structure you're introducing works. Be careful not to give the impression that what you're doing is something dreadful. The coin system worked for me after trial and error. You can find your own reward system.

The stage from 11 to 15 years old can be difficult. Children are entering their pre-teen and teen years. It may be that some of their friends do not have schedules or chore lists and they can sometimes have an influence on your child. This can lead to questions like, "Why do I have to do this," and expressions such as: "This is not fun" or "No one else in the universe has to follow a schedule." You may notice this is especially prominent if you are trying it for the first time. When children are small it is quite effortless, but at this stage it could be more problematic.

Most parents give up during these times. They don't want to deal with their children's attitudes, which hearkens back to what I said earlier about emotional parenting. This is an essential time in your child's life, even though they may be resisting structure and guidance. In fact, this is the time when they need it most. Whatever the case might be, make the price so inviting that they can only say yes! Perhaps it is time to change techniques and tactics. Maybe they outgrew the gold coins and now it's time to work together for one price: a trip, an extracurricular activity, the permission to have a cell phone, etc. You know your child, get creative! The goal here is to make it work! Involve them in the process of navigating the problem and finding a solution. This period is more about working together. You are still in control, but their input, views, and choices are important, too.

This calls for a more proactive approach. One way might be to sit together and work out a plan. Write down the things that are set and cannot be changed. For example, family worship, school, music, mealtimes, bed/wake time, reading, and family time. Then make a list of things that are important to your child such as personal time, talking on the phone, hobbies, or journaling. After that is set and communicated, make a list of daily activities that still need to be completed to have a productive and effective day. These might include chores, exercise, new projects, and good deeds. After this has been carefully analyzed, schedule downtime in the day for these activities. It is not so much about time as it is about a process of accomplishing what needs to be done. As soon as it is all done, your child will have more time for their own personal preferences, and they like that!

From 16 to 18 years of age, children are on automatic pilot. The concept of schedules is very much a part of their daily life; at this point, they may love to write up their own lists and see what they can accomplish. Accordingly, this is a good time to allow your child to write out their own schedules and to-do lists. They can write it on paper or on their phones, tablets, or computers. Give them that freedom. It will help them learn how to set reminders for themselves, which in turn helps them stay on track. Once a week in our house, we go over the children's to-do lists to make sure they are being accomplished. This period of life is easier, but it sets the tone for the transition into adulthood. Sometimes your child might feel as if they don't need a schedule anymore. You can feel free to extend the rope and see how much they can handle while remaining accountable to their weekly requirements. Still, you will need to communicate with them and offer guidance when needed.

Teens often realize that having a schedule is not a bad thing. Some will automatically work out their own schedules because they see that it brings organization and time management into their lives. Still, even as they get older, rewards and positive reinforcements remain important. Some ideas include gift cards, Amazon shopping, date night with mom or dad, summer camp/space camp, Broadway tickets, sports season tickets, cash app rewards, Zelle rewards, and school days off. These make for an awesome incentive and reward responsibility. Eventually, there comes a time where children do outgrow these incentives and simply do what they are expected to do because they know it is right. That day will come!

Work out each child's schedule individually. Your children are all different, as are their activities, responsibilities, and needs. This is not one size fits all. Remember that one of the beautiful things about homeschool is that your child is receiving personalized learning, and guidance. Here are examples of schedules that I have used with my children over the years. They are only here to give you a guide on how to set yours up:

CRUZ PRESCHOOL SCHEDULE

CHORES	MONDAY	TUESDAY	WEDNESDAY	THURSDAY	FRIDAY	SATURDAY	SUNDAY
MAKE BED							
BRUSH TEETH							
GET DRESSED							
BRUSH HAIR							
Breakfast							
FEED PETS							
PLAY TIME							
SET TABLE							
CHORES							
PUT TOYS AWAY							

Cruz Elementary School Schedule

Time	Task
8:00 am	Wake Up / Personal chores
8:30 am	Breakfast / Family worship
9:00 am	Chore #1
9:30 am	Personal Worship
9:45-10:00 am	Good deed
10-2:30 pm	School
2:30-3:00 pm	Lunch
3-4 pm	Music / Exercise (alternate)
4-4:30 pm	Hobby
4:30-5 pm	Read
5-6 pm	Music / exercise (alternate)
6:30 pm	Shower
7:00-8 pm	Dinner
8-9 pm	Free time
9-9:30 pm	Video/Family Worship
9:30 pm	Goodnight

Cruz Middle School/ High School Schedule

Time	Task
7:15 am	Wake Up
7:30 am	Personal Chores & Personal Worship
8:00 am	Chore #1
8:30 am	Breakfast / Family Worship
9-2:00 pm	School
2-2:30 pm	Hobby
2:30 pm	Lunch
3:00 pm	Read
3:30-4:30 pm	Music & exercise (alternate)
4:30-5:30 pm	Music & exercise (alternate)
5:30-6 pm	Shower
6-6:30 pm	Good deed
6:30-7:00 pm	Chore #2
7-8 pm	Dinner
8-9 pm	Free time
9-10 pm	Family time/ worship
10 pm	Goodnight

- Tuesday - Extracurricular activities all day
- Thursday - His Light co-op/support group all day
- Friday - Half a day Saints co-op group + half a day for make-up classes and preparation for Sabbath = Full day
- High school schedule time changes and gets revised once the child begins their shadowing and volunteer programs or dual enrollment at a community college or university. The core stays the same and they are still responsible for completing it.
- Kids will follow picture schedules from ages three to five for preschool.
- Each schedule spans from Monday to Friday.
- Saturdays are dedicated to church, family, and friends.
- Sunday is a fun day for the family and provides time to get organized for the week.

Rewards

Reading is extremely important. While we don't include it as part of the curriculum, we integrate it as part of the daily schedule. My children choose a book from the home library, and after they have read it completely, they are asked to turn in a small summary of the book. (I learned about this when reading Ben Carson's description of what his mother had him do as a child.) For each book read and report written, they received five dollars in elementary school and ten dollars in middle school and high school. They could read as many books as they liked. The only stipulation is that the books had to be chapter books of 100 pages or more. While we knew it could be costly, this keeps the motivation going and the benefits are endless.

Chores Example List

Chores rotate from child to child so everyone has the opportunity to learn and master every task.

Unit 3: Children's Daily Schedules and Routines

CRUZ WEEKLY CHORE CHART

MONDAY:
Sorting / doing / folding laundry
Grocery List
Meal Prep
Pick up mail
Change Bed Linens
Clean Bedroom

TUESDAY:
Water Plants
Pick up Mail
Clean bedroom

WEDNESDAY:
Drawer organizing
Closet reorganizing
Pick up mail
Clean Bedroom

THURSDAY:
Clean Bathrooms
Water plants
Pick up mail
Clean bedroom

FRIDAY:
Dusting   Vacuum/mop floors   Pick up Mail
Clean Car   Car Wash
Clean back/front porch   Clean bedroom

ACTION STEPS

"Tell me and I forget. Teach me and I remember. Involve me and I learn."
—Benjamin Franklin

Unit 4

CHARACTER BUILDING

Melody was a toddler when on a Sunday afternoon my husband and I went to the mall. The stores were very crowded and in the center of the mall there was an area for children to play. My husband thought it would be a good idea to let our daughter play and wait for me there, as I was still going about my shopping. As he sat and waited there with other parents watching their young ones, he noticed that a small child came over to our daughter and kicked her on her leg completely unprompted. He looked around for the parent of that child, looked at Melody, and saw her standing in disbelief. Not only did the child hit her once but she did it again. At this point, my husband went over to where Melody was standing with tears in her eyes. She said, "Papi, why did she hit me? I didn't do anything to her." The reality of this situation is that most parents think certain behaviors are normal because society sees them as normal. We will never know the parent of that child, but we do know one of two things happened: 1) If the parent was watching, they probably excused it as normal behavior for a toddler, or 2) the parent was not paying attention to their child. Whichever of the two it may have been, the truth of the matter is that we have more and more character issues with our children because parents have been desensitized to certain behaviors or they are simply not present to their children. It is important to see where we as parents sweep situations under the rug, hoping children acquire integrity of character as they grow, when in fact we need to teach it to them.

Parents are not focusing enough on character. This issue profoundly affects our children's behavior. I believe home education is an antidote and goes hand in hand with character building. This next chapter will give you the tools to build a good foundation of character, no matter how old your children may be. John Wooden has a quote that I love. He says, "Be more concerned with your character than your reputation." Why are our children suffering from a lack of character? Why is it so hard for them to have good patterns of behavior? Here is a simple answer. Children watch and imitate. Twenty seconds of television can impact the behavior of the viewer in ways that will take years to erase. In a culture where a child is watching over 20 hours of television per week, who is raising them? Technology has its assets, but we must be careful about how much unsupervised time we are giving our children. Another aspect of the problem is that parents do not have enough character themselves because it was not taught to them. Their parents also hoped that they would get it at school with teachers and other role models. However, the reality is that we cannot pass down a trait that we ourselves may not possess. Yet another factor that affects character building is peer pressure, whether it comes from family, friends, support groups, church, or school. Because parents are not focusing enough on this concept, we allow our social circles to unduly influence our children. Sometimes we let go for the simple reason that we don't want others to judge us and think that we are too rigid or strict. In reality, most parents wish they had children who would say please and thank you, be kind, have good moral values, obey, display self-control, share with others, and have a good work ethic, just to name a few. How do our children acquire these traits when our culture is teaching them differently?

Webster's Dictionary defines the word "character" as: one of the attributes or features that make up and distinguish an individual. In other words, our character is the mental and moral qualities we possess. It names the way someone thinks, feels, and behaves. I like to put it this way: Character is who we are when nobody's watching.

I've had, through the years, a profound responsibility as I am raising my children with this concept of character building. I want them to display authenticity and be genuine wherever they are, regardless of whether I am present or not. In other words, I desire for their character to be something that is independent of attempts to please us as parents or avoid punishment. I want their character to come from true conviction and from their hearts. So, who are they? Who are my children? Whom do they reflect? Those are the questions you need to ask yourself when deciding to work on your children's character. Making a fictional picture of who you want your children to become will help you find a way to get there. Remember character is built over time; it affects and determines behavior, and behavior needs to be taught.

There are many character traits, and a good way to start the process of building is by determining which character traits you want to instill in your children. Again, envision what you value with the end in mind.

Here is a list to get you started:

Obedience
Honesty/truthfulness
Hardworking
Stewardship
Discernment
Kindness
Responsibility
Self-control
Work ethic
Working with contentment
Good manners
Teamwork
Initiative
Servant's heart
Decision-making
Enthusiasm

Helping
Tolerance
Compassion
Loyalty
Confidence
Generosity
Courage
Conscientiousness
Ambition
Sincerity
Persistence
Attention to detail
Dependability
Time management
Discipline
Diligence
Compassion
Respect
Attentiveness
Gratitude
Virtue
Patience
Forgiveness
Punctuality
Hospitality
Boldness
Thriftiness
Wisdom

These are some of the character traits important to our family. But how do we acquire them when children feel entitled and certain behaviors seem to be so rooted in them? Or when children are older and they start to display patterns in their character that are not healthy for their success?

My son, Jason, was about 12 years old when he was playing basketball with some of his friends in the parking lot of our church. It had been brought to my attention that he was needed inside for a praise and worship rehearsal, and they were waiting for him and the others to start. I called him aside and said, "Jason, I understand that you'd much rather stay outside playing basketball with your friends, but you are committed to playing with the praise and worship band and they need you inside for rehearsal." He immediately told his friends, "Guys, I've gotta go" and he went inside. A dad of one of the boys that was also playing basketball was waiting for his son to go inside when he asked me, "How do you do it?" I asked, "Do what?" and he responded, "How do you get him to obey without getting mad or defiant? I waited until everyone went inside so I wouldn't have to deal with my son's attitude or misconduct," the father went on to say. That is a typical way parents deal with their children's character nowadays. They don't deal with the situation and hope it will change on its own. What character trait did Jason display? I could mention a few from my list: diligence, discipline, responsibility, but most importantly obedience. If you can teach obedience, you've won half the battle.

Children and teens need boundaries. But they also need to know what is expected of them ahead of time.

It was a Saturday night, and we were visiting with friends. There were about five girls sitting together chitchatting, giggling, and laughing as we moms did the same. I noticed that my daughter Melanie all of a sudden was left alone sitting on a small wooden bench not far from me. I saw one of the moms approach Melanie to ask her some questions. Not long after that, the mom came back and said to me, "You should be very proud of Melanie." I went over and asked my daughter why she was there alone and she replied, "I am not allowed to go to the bathroom without you, Mom, so I am waiting for them to come back." The other moms who were listening to our conversation then said, "I wish our daughters would do that! No matter how many times we tell them, they just go." And they laughed! What character trait was displayed here? Again, I could name a few: self-control, discernment, and discipline. But the one I would like to stress is obedience! Children as well as teens need to know where their boundaries lay and what is expected of them. It will not happen if you don't clarify the rules for them ahead of time. When the expectations are clear to them, they will know their destination and can make good choices.

Character training needs to be consistent and ongoing. Take the character trait that you want to instill or change in your child and work on it for 21 days, consistently throughout your day. It is the consistency that will get you the results you need.

Now, understand that being consistent requires time, effort, creative energy, determination, help from other sources, change, and repetition. You must be willing to commit to it, strive for excellence, and be the example. Children are our purpose, and what we have envisioned for them takes an enormous amount of work to bring about. This brings me to my next point.

We need the proper tools. Get help for yourself from books, training, mentors, personal coaches, and character-building curriculums. Then get extra help for your children and choose a method that is good for all ages. You can look for books that you can read as a family, discussions after movies is a wonderful tool, as well as audio and everyday life situations that display the character trait you are working on. Do not criticize or put your children down when they fail. You are not seeking out the bad, you are praising and recognizing the good. You are intentionally working toward the vision of your result. Dream with me of having children who internally and externally portray good character traits. Be proactive!

When Melody started college as a senior in high school through the dual enrollment program, we wanted her to have this experience while still at home. As parents, we were concerned about the fact that she would encounter situations, people, and decisions that would challenge her at a particularly young age. We realized that she would have to be with nonbelievers and remain resolute in her faith. My husband and I were very aware of what this could entail, but we also knew we had given her a good foundation and built her character on a strong set of values. Being in a classroom with people of different ethnic backgrounds, political views, Christian beliefs, social classes, ages, and moral codes, with a professor who was an atheist was not exactly what we were hoping for in her introduction to college life. Nevertheless, if you ask Melody today, she will tell you that Humanities 101 was her favorite class and her atheist teacher, her favorite professor. She was faithful and true when no one was watching. That is the end in mind. Bear in mind, it wasn't always easy. We had a lot of bumps along the way, but I want to encourage you that it can be done! Boundaries, persistence, and the appropriate tools will allow you to succeed and build children of character.

Below, you will find some character-building supplemental help. I have used these resources and found them helpful with my kids. After every episode, show, book, and audio segment, we left time for discussion to answer the question, "What character trait can we learn from this?"

Books:

- Bible
- Biographies: Tim Tebow, Condoleezza Rice, Ben Carson, Colin Powell, Joni Eareckson Tada, David Livingstone
- Others: *Before You Meet Prince Charming* by Sarah Mally, *Game Changer* by Kirk Cousins, *The Richest Caveman* by Doug Batchelor, *A Girl's Guide to Making Really Good*

Choices by Elizabeth George, *A Boy's Guide to Making Really Good Choices* by Jim George, *Live Original* by Sadie Robertson, *The Pilgrim's Progress* by John Bunyan, *I Am Malala* by Malala Yousafzai

Movies/Shows:

- *Gifted Hands*; *Little House on the Prairie*; *Where the Red Fern Grows*; *The Andy Griffith Show*; *Highway to Heaven*; *The Blind Side*; *McFarland, USA*; *Anne of Green Gables*; *Little Women*; *Swiss Family Robinson*

Audio:

- *Adventures in Odyssey, Your Story Hour*
- Curriculum: Character First Education (highly recommended)

Unit 4: Character Building

ACTION STEPS

"Intelligence plus character—that is the goal of true education."
—*Martin Luther King Jr.*

Unit 5

HOW TO TAKE CARE OF WHAT MATTERS MOST (YOU)

I have a passion for homeschooling, and motherhood is what I love the most. With that said, I must tell you that I have not always taken care of myself. I am a giver by nature, and to me it is all or nothing. This means I tend to go on and on until I face exhaustion and burnout. Maybe this is not the case with you, but I am sure that sometime in your life after having children, caring for them full-time, and adopting a homeschool lifestyle, you have run low on energy or wished you had more time for yourself. This is not a bad thing! But we feel guilty as moms for even having such thoughts. Self-care is not selfish. I learned this the hard way. In order to care for the most important people in your life, you must take care of yourself. I am sure this does not come easy for you either because for the most part, moms give and give. In this unit, I will show you how to take care of yourself, how to renew your strengths, to recharge, and stop running around in circles. Doesn't that sound amazing? Earlier, I told you that homeschooling must meet the needs of your child in three areas: physical, mental, and spiritual. Well, it works the same for us moms. I invite you to indulge in this unit of the book and if no one has told you lately, let me be the first. YOU MATTER! I want to encourage you to stop what you are doing and read this next chapter sipping on some good tea, lemonade, coffee, or hot cocoa. Stop reading! Go get your drink ready and don't forget a cozy blanket. Come back to enjoy and learn how to take care of what matters most. YOU!

Why do I say what matters most is you? It sounds self-centered, proud, selfish, and almost makes you feel uncomfortable, right? In reality, you are what matters most to your children and if you are not taking care of yourself properly, you are not taking care of them properly. That would not be fair to them or to the people around you. God entrusted our children to us because he knew that we would be the best moms for them. But when we are neglecting ourselves, we are neglecting them.

In this unit, I will show you how to do everything you need to do without burning out. I will give you illustrations and share ideas that have worked for me through trial and error over the course of many years. These are things that can help you get rid of the guilt of having to do everything and be everything to everyone. This chapter can help you live your best and give your best depending on the season of your life you are living. So, lets jump in.

One essential thing is to take time for yourself guilt free and stay away from the mentality of, "If I don't do it, then who will?"

More and more, I hear the following words from young and older moms alike: "I am so tired," "I am burnt out," and "If I only had a few minutes to myself." The truth of the matter is that the only minutes we get to be alone are often when we go to the bathroom. Even then, I remember leaving the door slightly ajar just in case something happened. How many of you are guilty of taking a shower with the baby strapped in the car seat on the other side of the shower curtain, peeking every two minutes to make sure they're okay? I know I am not the only one that has done this crazy thing. I am not talking about a sacrificial mentality. This was or is a reality for a lot of us. And while it is true that there is a season that requires more of us, it is only a season. So, what does it take for us to take ourselves seriously? What series of events must happen in our lives for us to say, "I need to take care of me."

At times, it feels like the more we give of ourselves, the more we are expected to give. Having one child is the equivalent of having a full-time job and most of us have more than one, a house to run, homeschooling, extracurricular activities, church or social obligations, and extended family members to oversee. What's more, some of you moms work full-time or part-time jobs outside of the home. Then how are we supposed to take care of ourselves when the list of responsibilities can go on and on and just thinking about it makes you want to give up. You feel guilty because you believe you are doing something wrong by taking care of yourself when you have so many responsibilities on your plate. In reality, you need to take care of yourself so you can take care of everything and everyone around you. What fills you? What do you enjoy doing? What do you wish you had time for? Be honest! Don't feel bad, take a moment to think. I will teach you how to honor yourself in this part of the book. First and foremost, it starts with taking care of your spirit.

Empowering Your Soul

Spiritual Life

I remember leaving the hospital with my husband, feeling devastated after hearing the doctor say, "I am sorry, you've just miscarried." I was crying as I experienced the loss of the pregnancy I had been looking forward to for the previous four years. It was one of the hardest experiences of my life. I felt as if my heart had been left at the hospital and no one could give me answers. I heard comments like, "You are going to be okay," "It wasn't meant to be," "Your body knows why, better now than later," and "Keep trying, you'll get pregnant again. Miscarriages are very common." I could continue with the list of unwanted remarks. As I got home and lay in my bed numb as my heart pounded, I heard my cell ring. It was my doctor saying, "Please come back, your pregnancy levels are still going up and we don't know why." I remember getting back in my car and praying for a miracle. Oh, how I wanted it to be true. How I wanted to still be pregnant and have my baby.

See, my husband and I had done things right. We married young, graduated from college, bought our first home, and now it was time to start our family. So, I wrestled with the "why" and gave God every reason for having this baby. This, only to hear the doctor tell me after a sonogram that I had to go to the operating room due to an ectopic pregnancy. I wanted to know what that meant but by the look on his face I knew it wasn't good. He said it was a miracle that my tube had not burst yet. I saw a worried look in my husband's eyes, so I knew there was more to it. You see, as a result of this complication I would only have one healthy tube, which meant it would be harder for me to conceive again. As I went home the next day after the surgery, the only thing I had to hold on to was God. As a child, I had accepted Jesus into my life and made him my Lord and Savior. I've always loved God and made Him Lord of my life when I made a decision to baptize and to follow Him. I've never been one to doubt God and His plans for my life, but this time was different. This situation had tested every fiber in me and now I needed Him more than ever before. If you've ever experienced something like this you know that your boss, your friends, your family expect you to bounce back as if nothing had ever happened. You may try, but in reality you have a sorrow inside of you that won't leave. It was then when I truly realized the need for spiritual intervention. All my life I had done things the "right" way at the "right" time, but now things were out of my control and all I could hold onto was Jesus. That is when the hymn, "I Need Thee Every Hour" took on a different meaning in my life. At times, I felt like I could not breathe and the only way to make it to the next hour was by depending on the One who had created me. I don't know if you have ever felt like this, if you have a similar story, or if you feel like this now. But let me tell you, I held on tight and I never let Him go. This situation taught me that you can do all the right things, belong to the right church, come from a Christian family, but if you are not depending on Jesus every hour and every minute, you will lose it and things will not go right for you. I would have cheated you if I told you that I did it any other way. I don't want to change my story so people can read my book. I don't want to leave this portion out and pretend that it was by my own means and my own creative mind that I got this far. It has been by needing Him every hour and depending on Him every minute.

Taking care of your spiritual needs is a must for survival. You see, I believe that we are spiritual beings and if we don't connect to our source daily, we will not have the power to push through. So how do you connect daily in the busyness of your everyday life? I have expressed to you from the beginning of this book that all these ideas have been tested by me because I can only give you what has worked in my life. With that said, always keep in mind that you are an individual so you must do what works for you. How do you start? You need to be intentional about what you receive and what you give, and this begins the moment you wake up.

- God's Word - Hold God's word in your heart and mind so when situations arise you can avail yourself of His promises, His council, and His grace because you recognize His voice. Spend time daily memorizing His word. Here is a practical way. Find a passage or a verse each week. I found that BibleGateway is a wonderful source. Copy and paste this verse and make at least five copies. Cut them in strips and tape them in places that you frequent a lot during the day. For example, on the bathroom mirror, on the refrigerator door, in the laundry room, on your night lamp, or on the steering wheel of your car. As you pass by these areas, repeat the scripture in your mind. By the end of the week, you will have memorized God's word and written it in your heart.

- Bible Study - I am not a morning person! I would often hear about my friends who wake up at 5 AM to spend time with the Lord. Just the thought of that puts added stress in my life. How could I add one more thing to my day if I can barely deal with what is on my plate? The reality is that the Lord knows what season of life you are living right now. He is not asking for a 5 AM commitment that you can't keep. I understand you! I have been there so many times. But better than that, He understands you. So, let me give you some ideas that you could incorporate at different stages of your life. This is the only way I have been able to keep my spiritual plate full and nourish my family's spiritual needs at the same time. We are created body, soul, and spirit, so we should commit minutes to meeting those needs.

When my children were young, early in the morning, before my routines started and while the kids were still asleep, I made my coffee and sat on my front porch to eat from God's word. I often wondered if my neighbors thought I was crazy. Some of them would wave as they drove off to work. At times, my kids woke up earlier than expected and looked out the front window to find me studying. They knew mommy was spending time alone with God and didn't interrupt. Now that my kids are older, they give me that uninterrupted special time as well. They know that God comes first.

One of my favorite ways of reconnecting with God is through Bible study: research, reading, and meditation. Make it a daily habit and see how God can change you for the better. Pick only one book to study and work on it, dig deep, and see how God can minister in your life and reveal Himself to you. Listen to Bible audiobooks on your headphones and multitask while going about your day.

Another tool that I used was reading the entire Bible in one year with my children. For Christmas, I often bought Bibles with the appropriate translation given the ages of my children and read it with them in one year cover to cover. When the children were small, I used *The Word and Song Bible*. When they were a little older, we used *The Children's Bible in 365 Stories*, and when they were teenagers we used *The One Year Bible NLT*. When we avail ourselves of tools like these, not only are we benefiting ourselves as moms, we are also benefitting our children. Another wonderful resource for Bible study is *The Busy Mom's Guide to Bible Study* by Lisa Whelchel. This book will help you dig deep into God's word in just 15 minutes. Some of my other favorites include *Ten Women of the Bible* by Max Lucado, *Well-Watered Women*, and *The Daily Grace Co*. These books can empower and nourish your soul daily. Remember, the more you do, the richer your life will be.

- Prayer Journal - I listened to Steve Harvey, a Christian comedian, for a motivational talk once and he said something that impacted me, "You have none because you ask not." He continued his talk by telling a fictional story, which I am going to paraphrase in my own words, that has stayed with me for many years. He said that someone went to heaven and as they were getting a heavenly tour, they saw a big container full of presents inside. The person asked, "What is this?" and the person giving the tour answered, "Those are all your blessings, but since you didn't ask for them, they are still in there." Matthew 7:7 says, "Ask and it will be given to you, seek and you will find, knock and the door will be open." Needless to say, many years ago I adopted the technique of writing down my prayer requests, my answered prayers, and my gratitude. And I take comfort in knowing what he says in Matthew 28:20, "I am with you ALWAYS."

- Prayer Partners - I have the sweetest prayer partner. She is an older lady from my church. When my older daughter went to college, she came up to me and asked me if I wanted to be her prayer partner. She would pray for my kids and in return I would pray for her son. Every morning at 5:00 AM, I get a text that simply reads, "prayed." When I wake up a little later, I return the text, "prayed." What comfort I feel knowing that someone is praying for my kids daily. She always prays first and lets me know as a reminder of our promise to each other. She holds me accountable and we bring each other's children to the Lord daily. Find yourself a prayer partner, a confidant, a woman of faith, someone who speaks truth to the Father on your behalf every day and someone for whom you will do the same.
- Prayer Walk - This idea started when my children were very young. I would put them in the stroller and take them for a stroll in the mornings. During this time, I would talk to God. There is something special about God and nature that helps you maintain focus throughout the day. A half an hour is all it would take to get the kids outdoors, get some vitamin D, and spend time in prayer. After the kids got older and could stay home alone for half an hour, I continued with this routine. No distractions, no texting, no talking on the phone. Just me and my God connecting and reconnecting. One day, before I started my morning prayer walk, I received some unpleasant news about a health issue I was facing. I

went on my daily walk and, as I was talking to my God, He gave me reassurance that everything was going to be okay. I looked up to the heavens to find my strength and saw an airplane writing with smoke in the air. I stopped to see what the writing said. It read, "Everything will be alright." I wish I could have taken a picture to show my family, and I wish I had a picture to print in this book so you could see it. But all I could do at that moment was kneel on the sidewalk and praise God in thankfulness for what I had just witnessed as the letters gently faded away. God had just spoken to me and it was going to be alright! And it was. Where is your quiet place? Where do you go to stay sane? Where is your hiding place? Where do you restore your soul? Where do you listen to God? Where do you get the answers you need?

- Talk to God All Day - It is true that we are extremely busy all day. And once the day begins, it can feel like a treadmill that does not stop. You spend your day directing and redirecting, teaching, and sometimes it feels like you are repeating yourself over and over, day in and day out. One of the ways that I have kept my thoughts on the right track is by talking to God all day and asking for His wisdom in everything that I do. If I am teaching, I ask Him to teach me. If I am doing laundry, I ask Him to wash away my sins. If I am organizing, I ask Him to organize my path. If I am exercising, I ask Him to make my body the temple for the Holy Spirit. Pray over every room in the house as you walk in and out of them. You get my point, right? Now you understand how my life depends on it. I matter enough that I need to take care of myself spiritually. This practice might look different for you, but remember that these are ideas to help you take care of yourself. We are spiritual beings, and we need to stay connected to spiritual power. By talking to God all day, you are staying connected to your life source and I promise you will not feel like you are doing life alone.

- Mom Prayer Time - Once a week for six years, I had the privilege to meet with beautiful and spiritual moms for prayer. As our children played near us, 15 of us met on Thursday mornings at 10:45 AM for 15 minutes of prayer and fellowship. What an amazing experience this became. We brought our joys, happinesses, concerns, frustrations, and worries before the Lord. As friends, we prayed for one another, encouraged one another, cried with each other, and shared our answered prayers with one another. All it took was 15 minutes out of our day, but there were countless blessings. It was also a wonderful example for our toddlers, young children, preteens, and teens to witness on a weekly basis. If you don't belong to a prayer group, I invite you to find or start one. Only 15 minutes a week can restore your soul, push you back in the right direction, lift your spirits, and bring peace. Knowing that you have a group of friends praying with you will give you the strength to carry on.

- Praise - From an early age, praise has been an integral part of my life. It is essential to acknowledge and give reverence to the supernatural. When our children were born, we decided that we wanted them to praise, too—to declare with their mouth, hands, and body their love and thankfulness to their savior. But what better way to teach than to live by example. Why do we need to praise? Praise, according to the *Macmillan Dictionary*, means "to express warm approval or admiration of." I have saved this section for last because it sums up the steps of empowering our souls as a means of being whole and taking care of ourselves. We matter to whom? We matter to God, our creator! And in response we live a life of praise, expressing our approval and our admiration. Praise is not optional. It is not what you give to God when you go to church because everyone else is doing it. It is not what you do once in a while when you have time or inspiration. Praise is a necessary component of your life. Here are a few ideas on how praise can be incorporated into your busy life. I have discovered in my life that praise is just as much about me as it is about God. It requires total surrender and humility in the face of something bigger than me.

- Play Praise - In the morning when you and your children rise, play praise music. It is so much easier with Google Home or Alexa nowadays. YouTube also has an amazing selection of praise that you could play on your television set. Play Christian radio, CDs, satellite radio in the car as you are driving from place to place. Scripture songs gave my family an opportunity to sing and memorize scripture at the same time. Play praise as the day is winding down right before family time to give the kids the heads-up that the day begins with praise and ends with praise.

- Physical Praise - Lift your hands, sing His praises, praise His name with dancing, as in Psalms 149:3. Kneel when you pray, proclaim His promises, His mercies, and His goodness. And don't forget to enter His gates with thanksgiving and praise in corporal worship.
- Praise with Instruments - It is important to my family that we use our musical talents for praising the Lord. My husband plays the piano and trumpet and has always used his talent for praising God. When we started dating, one of the things that drew us together was our shared love of praise and using our talents for God. Some people are born with a special talent, but others like us multiply our talents by virtue of God's grace and power. He gives us the talent. My husband played and I sang in the praise choir at church for many years. We even had a praise and worship band that traveled around the country praising God. We most definitely wanted to pass this on to our children and make praise a priority in their lives. So, each one of them got to pick two instruments of their choice, learn them well, and offer them to God in praise. Melody plays the piano and guitar, Jason plays the violin and bass guitar and added cello on his own.

Melanie plays the piano and the ukulele, and they all sing. Let me encourage you to give yourself and your families in praise to the Lord. Make your homes a place of worship.

Taking Care of Your Body

I was sitting on my front porch having my morning coffee and reading, as is my routine before the start of a new day. This particular morning, I had finished my time with God and I was doing some personal reading to enhance my life. As I was finishing the chapter that I was on, the author said to close the book, stop your reading, and schedule that doctor appointment you have been putting off. You see, I felt as if God was talking to me through the book. I had been putting off going to the gynecologist for some time. But that day was different. I stood up from my rocking chair, grabbed my cell, and scheduled the appointment. As moms, we have the tendency to put everyone and everything in front of our personal needs and we must get out of that mentality. We don't have the option not to take care of ourselves. The day came for my appointment and the doctor examined me as usual. Just before he said his usual parting words, "Great seeing you. I'll see you next year," he told me, "Take this prescription and get a mammogram done." I replied, "Is there a problem?" and he answered, "Normally, mammograms are done at 40, but I would like you to get one done as soon as possible." I left his office concerned. Time went on and I ignored it hoping it was no big deal but in the back of my mind I knew I had to get it done. I eventually worked up my courage and made an appointment for my first mammogram ever.

If the unpleasantness of the machine is not enough, the room is extremely cold and the person doing the exam is usually far from friendly. You try to read their expressions, but you can't. I tried asking if everything was fine and the nurse replied, "The doctor will be in shortly." I can relive the experience just by thinking about it. My heart rate started to rise, my palms started to sweat, my body started to tremble and I could feel myself freeze, waiting for the doctor. When he finally returned, he said, "We have found a lump in your breast and recommend going to a specialist." These are not the words you are hoping to hear from your doctor. As I left the hospital, a million and a half thoughts came to my mind and none of them positive. I drove into a Walmart parking lot and began to sob as I never had before. You see, I had three small children at the time. This was not the right time, I kept on telling God.

It is never the right time! Moms, we don't have the luxury to not take proper care of ourselves and this brings me to the point in this book where I am going to tell you the same words that saved my life: get up and schedule that appointment you've been putting off! You don't have the choice not to do it. Believe me, I had the same martyr mentality and the same excuses. I get it, I've been there where you give everyone their vitamins and forget yours, where you feed everyone and lose your appetite, where you fill your children's water bottles but don't even think about drinking yours.

It was early in the morning when I was getting ready to leave with the children to the homeschool support group. Everyone was dressed, lunches were done, and bookbags were in the van. I was walking towards the hallway and suddenly, as I turned to pick up my sweater from the bed, I was overcome by excruciating pain in my lower back. I screamed at the kids to come help me. I did not know what was going on. My husband was away for work in Chicago, my parents were away at meetings in Orlando, and I was immobile on top of the bed. I would like you to know that I am for the most part a very healthy person. I didn't know whether to call the rescue or wait and see if the pain would pass. Again, my first thought was, "This is not the right time. I can't leave the kids alone and I have no time to get sick. Not now, Lord. Today is not the day, not while my husband is away." At that moment, I asked my son to call a friend who lived a short distance from our house and whose children also attended the same homeschool group. My hope was that if she was home, she could come and pick up my kids and take them with her while this pain would leave and I could go about my day. Things did not happen exactly as I'd prayed for. I managed to get in the car after the kids had left and drive to the hospital, praying that every traffic light would turn green so I wouldn't have to stop. In excruciating pain, I made it to the ER to hear the doctor tell me, "You have a kidney stone." It was the worst pain I have ever experienced! Have you been there? I hope not! Taking care of our bodies is a MUST. Self-care is not optional! We must be intentional when we take care of our body, mind, and spirit. If you are fine, then everyone around you will be fine. Here are some of my recommendations that might work for you.

- Make a list of all your personal appointments. These may include physical examinations, blood tests, mammograms, pap smears, and annual gynecological, dental, and vision checkups. Schedule them during your birthday month and remember that month is dedicated to taking care of you. Another idea is to do it at the beginning of the year because most insurance policies renew for the new year, giving you a clean slate. But either way, you have a whole year before you need to go back again.
- Drink water: Keep plastic water bottles handy and visible. Make sure you know how many ounces and how many bottles you need daily. My suggestion is that you do not throw the bottles away after you drink them so you can keep a proper count. Place your water bottle in the same place all the time so you can come back to it. Find a routine that works for you. I drink a bottle of water with lemon first thing in the morning and I have a water intake app on my phone that keeps me on track.
- Take your vitamins: Do your yearly blood examination. This will be a good indicator of how your health is and if there are any supplements missing. If everything is fine, then a multivitamin or a food supplement will be enough for you. Make a habit of taking them at the same time every day. If your children are taking vitamins, this is a good time for everyone to do it together.
- Rest: I can't remember the last time I had a good night's rest. So typical of us moms. My husband has the talent to put his head on the pillow and fall asleep right away.

Oh, how I wish that was the case for me. But there is something about us moms that when we feel the house is quiet and everyone is asleep, we start working. And we fall in the trap of going to bed past midnight most nights, making it impossible to wake up in the mornings. From the time the babies are born, we become sleep deprived. We often read in books and hear other experts say, sleep when the baby is sleeping. But let's face it, in reality that hardly ever happens. So, we are physically tired all the time. Why is sleep important and how do we address this deficit? Your body needs rest and sleep to function at its best. There are many neurological benefits to getting the proper amount of rest and a few of them are you will be more productive, you will make better decisions, you will be more alert, and you will have better self-control—all the things needed to have a good homeschool day! You may already know that we sleep in cycles of 90 to 110 minutes. So, when our sleep is constantly interrupted, the brain cannot optimize its potential. Another point I would like to stress is the importance of not hitting the snooze button. Figure out how many hours of sleep you need in order to be well rested and feel at your best. Then make sure to get those hours, and when it is time to get up do not hit that snooze button and continue to sleep. If you do, your brain will enter into another sleep cycle, which means that when the alarm goes off again and you have to wake up, your brain thinks that it needs to continue to sleep. That is why you feel tired and sleepy.

Place your alarm or your phone in another room of the house, which forces you to get up. I promise if you do this for 21 days straight, your body will adjust to this new behavior, giving you a more productive and better day. Your body will have also rejuvenated during the night because it got adequate rest.

Beautify Yourself

At the very least, change out of your pajamas! There is nothing more comfortable and relaxing than wearing a pair of pajamas. And so, before you know it, it is four in the afternoon and you are still wearing them. Take this advice. CHANGE! Once you are out of bed, beautify yourself.

We often confuse the need to maintain our beauty with vanity. However, in reality, one has nothing to do with the other. Homeschool moms begin to develop a reputation at times for self-carelessness. Close your eyes and tell me what you see when you think of a homeschool mom. Old pajamas, no makeup, long jean skirt, oversized T-shirt, sandals, long hair, no manicure or pedicure. Why is that? Is it because we have no time? Or a sense of style? Is it because we are always taking care of others and forget about ourselves? Let me help you change that pattern. Regardless of whether you are on a budget, every woman likes to feel beautiful, so at the very least do this:

- Once a week, do a face mask (coffee grounds work well)
- Cut your nails short and apply a clear coat

- Find a beauty school and get your eyebrows and mustache waxed
- Buy a bra that fits (get measured)
- Throw away your grandma underwear
- Buy underwear without panty lines
- Change your hairstyle (find one that you can style and maintain yourself)
- Buy yourself a cute water bottle and a pretty phone case
- Stop for coffee
- Buy a bouquet of flowers for yourself or pick them from your garden
- Show your legs once in a while
- Read a good book
- Make a pampering wish list (your husband will appreciate it)
- Get a homeschool life coach
- Have your own professional photoshoot

These few tips will give you and others a different perspective of a beautiful, well-put-together homeschool mom and it will make a difference in terms of how you feel about yourself. Give yourself a little pampering time, because you matter!

Eating Healthy

I don't have a story about how I lost weight by eating healthy. I've never had a weight issue so that is not what this portion of the book is about. Although that has not been my situation, poor eating habits have been. You've heard the saying that it is not the outside that counts, but the inside. Well, they are right because in my case the outside is slim, but the inside is needing a change. That change came when I had my firstborn, and I knew that the eating habits I had were not what I wanted for her. Here is an example of what a typical day looked like for me. Breakfast (coffee) on the go. Coke at 10 AM for energy, a Cuban tostada at noon for lunch (I am Cuban, and a tostada consists of white Cuban bread loaded with butter), and dinner with my husband in the evenings. Somehow, I got a reputation that I didn't like to eat and therefore food was not important to me. That was not the case at all. Since I didn't naturally gain weight, I didn't focus on the repercussions these poor choices could have later years. Right up to my marriage, since I lived with my parents my mom took care of all our meals at home or I ate on the go, and now that I was married and I had to do it on my own, it was not a priority. I always thought that if I was slim, I was good to eat anything. Boy, was I ever wrong. You could be five feet one and weigh 115 pounds and suffer from health issues and a lack of energy. You could be 160 pounds, feel overweight, and be just fine. I was using sugars and carbohydrates for energy because I had none myself. I knew things had to change because these were not the choices I wanted to pass down to my children. So, I started to educate myself and gradually changed. Let me give you some tips that helped me adopt healthy eating habits and create similar habits for my children.

- Fruits and vegetables should be visible - They should be handy, ready to grab and go. Wash them ahead of time so they are ready to eat. When the children are small, introduce fruits and vegetables weekly; give them a chance to get used to the taste. When they are older, have them as a part of their snacks and yours, too. In our case, we have fruits first thing in the morning.
- Healthy snacks - If you like snacking, have healthy snacks around and accessible. It is not about taking away yummy food. It is about eating the right food.
- Moderation and self-control - Train yourself to eat in moderation. One of the things that has helped me is to visually measure my portions and exercise self-control. I know that a fist of anything is enough for me, so I try to stay within that range. In this way, I am able to eat a wide variety of things without going overboard.
- Give yourself permission to cheat - Saturdays are a special day in our home because they are the day when we allow ourselves to have yummy dessert and treat ourselves to foods that we normally do not have during the week. We look forward to eating and eating out on Saturday nights.
- Eating at home - I have noticed that if we eat at home, we are more in control of what we eat and how much we eat. We have our Taco Tuesdays and our Saturday night dining out but other than that, we tend to eat at home. This really helps us stay balanced and form good eating habits.

- Keep it simple - Maintain a healthy balance of protein, carbohydrates, whole wheat, nuts, fruits, and vegetables and you will be on the right track.
- Plan your menu - Plan for success, grocery shop with a purpose, and be proactive in your decision to keep your family and yourself healthy. Things don't happen by chance. If you and your family want to have healthy eating habits, you must plan ahead. Make a grocery list with different menus for the week. Involve your family in the process. I often ask my kids, "What would you like to eat this week?" And we go around making sure that everyone has a meal they really like for that week with the proper nutritional values.

I am not the best cook. This gift does not come naturally to me. But I believe that the habits we instill in our children are habits they will have as adults. So, I've made it a point to learn and follow recipes. I'll let you in on a little secret: If you ask my children, they will tell you they love my cooking and that fills my heart with joy.

Exercise

This is an area in which I feel challenged. It doesn't come naturally to me and I don't like it. When I was in high school, I would do anything possible to get out of gym class. Once I entered college, drama, music, and reading were my clubs and hobbies. You would never find me exercising or playing a sport. Because

I've always had a slender build and a petite body frame, in my ignorance I never ascribed any importance to exercise and its positive benefits, including the positive outcomes it can have on mental and physical health. I knew I had to make changes, not because I came to enjoy exercise, but because I needed it.

Exercise reduces anxiety and depression, and it improves self-esteem and energy. Who doesn't need or want that? Like me, you may think, "I am not the exercise type and I have no time." I get it, but let me encourage you. We need to increase our heart rate and get our blood moving. Start with just 15 minutes a day. The exercise I am talking about here is not to lose those extra pounds (although that helps) or gain muscle and tone our bodies (although that is also great). It is the exercise that promotes long-term health, the kind that helps release stress and gives us a sense of well-being. Here are some helpful hints for incorporating 15 minutes of exercise in your daily routine to help you be a better you.

- Everything is better with a friend. Call a friend and have an exercise date. This is a great way to hold each other accountable.
- Put on your exercise clothes and shoes first thing in the morning.
- Exercise while the kids are outside or at the park. Many parks have a walking trail with exercise machines. This is a good way to take advantage of your time.
- Give yourself a 30-day challenge. Work against your own nature.

- Join a three-mile run. This is a great way to stay motivated and train for a good cause.
- Make it a part of your vision board. In this way, it is a constant reminder to get it done.
- Make a calendar for exercise. Change your exercise routine often to keep it interesting. This could include swimming, kickboxing, trampoline, bicycle, treadmill, walking outdoors, racquetball, tennis, or joining a gym. Any of these activities will give you a different perspective and you will feel better almost immediately.

Expand Your Mind

I am sure you've heard the phrase, "I feel like I am losing my mind," or you have even experienced it for yourself. Well, I'm sure you have! From the moment you wake up to the moment you go to bed, you are giving of yourself and meeting demands. You are always making sure everything runs as it is supposed to, smoothly and efficiently. When does your personal growth occur? When do you graduate from the daily demands of everyone around you to work on you? So often we neglect this part of our lives and find ourselves in bitterness, anxiety, self-pity, worry, self-doubt, and resentment. We must take care of our mental health every day, at least 15 minutes a day. In order to get to the next level and not lose your mind, you need to expand your mind. You deserve it! Remember, this is about working on you a little bit every day. Let me help you get to that level. Here are some practical ideas:

- Read - For Christmas, give yourself the books you would like to read the following year. Look for best sellers, ask your friends what they recommend, self-examine and pinpoint the areas of growth that you want for yourself and your family. Have those books accessible and ready to read. Focus on one book at a time. Don't overwhelm yourself with big chunks; small bites are better. You can find time while you wait at soccer practice, while kids are taking music lessons, while waiting for an appointment, while kids are napping, or even before you go to bed. Audiobooks are another excellent alternative that can assist you while you cook, do house chores, exercise, or go walking.
- Research a subject - Give yourself time to research something and become an expert in that area.
- Current events - Take the time to inform yourself about what is going on in the world, with the economy, with election candidates, world issues, and your city or your community.
- Take a course or pick up a new skill - YouTube offers a variety of free classes. Online courses are very accessible nowadays. Maybe you've always wanted to learn how to play an instrument, create an herb or flower garden, take up sewing, or take on a new hobby like photography, calligraphy, cake decoration, card making, or pottery.
- Cooking class - Maybe cooking has not been your forte. Expand your knowledge by taking a cooking class or attending a cooking show. Make a family recipe book to

keep those dishes and desserts as part of your family for years to come.
- Continue your education - Remember, what you are living right now looks like a lifetime but is only but a season of your life. What happens after this season is over? Are you preparing for that time? Stay in touch with the field you studied in college. Keep your certifications up to date and take any courses if needed. If your children are older and you have the time, work on that master's degree or take courses in a desired field of study.

Have Fun

You have often heard, "There is time for everything and a season for every activity under the heavens" (Ecclesiastes 3:1). Well, that is correct. There is even time to have fun, laugh, and enjoy life. So often, we say "that is on my bucket list" or "I'll get to that later," forgetting that the best time is now. When was the last time your children saw you laughing and having fun? Even worse, sometimes we can't remember the last time we had a complete conversation with our children that didn't involve a command or a reprimand. So often, they see us stressed out, rigid, authoritative, in control, or stern. They see tears in our eyes and feel our worry, but what about taking the time to have a little bit of fun every day? Let me remind you of some of the positive attributes of laughter and why it is so good for us. Laughter relaxes the whole body. It also boosts the immune system, triggers endorphins (the body's natural feeling good chemicals), protects the heart, and burns calories. In short, laughter could help you live longer. But how do you find time to have fun? Write down all the things that you would like to do for fun, put them on your vision board, and schedule them on your calendar. It can be as simple as a picnic or as daring as skydiving. Give yourself permission to enjoy life and do things that bring you joy and laughter. Here are a few fun and simple ideas of wholesome mom fun.

- Comedy club with friends
- Karaoke night
- Mom's night out
- Outdoor movie night
- Bake-off contest
- Game night
- Go out with the family, lower the windows of the minivan, play music really loud, and sing your hearts out (a family favorite)
- Take an unexpected outing
- Non-alcoholic happy hour
- Spend the night in a hotel just for fun
- Pay for someone's meal at the drive-through lane
- Cookie-decorating class
- Dog birthday party for the neighborhood dogs
- Family joke night
- Ask your children for a fun activity they would like to do
- Barbeque and water balloon Sunday fun day
- Cooking contest

It is amazing how creative we can become when we are intentional about doing things that are good for us. It is so important for our children to see us enjoying life because they are a part of it. They tend to model what they see. If you think about it, the best memories of your childhood were probably when your family was laughing and having fun together.

Unit 5: How to Take Care of What Matters Most (YOU)

ACTION STEPS

"An empty lantern provides no light. Self-care is the fuel that allows your light to shine brightly."
—*Unknown*

Unit 6

HOW TO KEEP IT ALL TOGETHER

You are probably mentally exhausted by now, wondering how you are going to incorporate all of this into your lifestyle and keep it all together. Remember, these are just ideas for you to pull from so that you can have a well-rounded and effective homeschool lifestyle that works for you.

The way that I have been able to pull it all together is by getting manic about being organized. Yes, I learned some of it from my childhood, but as you formulate your own lifestyle you need to make sure you come up with your own system. I am not obsessed with schedules and routines, but I have found that in order to stay on track and achieve my end goal, I must follow and incorporate organizational skills. It is true that you can find lots of websites, courses, and seminars on this subject, but I will share with you a set of schedules that have worked for me so that when you do your own homework, you have a guide. What I am about to share with you is based on my own research and trial and error. I know I say this over and over, but you need to find what works for you. Be balanced and flexible when need be.

Just like the kids have their schedule, you have yours. Write down everything that is important to you. I have found that 15-minute increments throughout the day work best for me. Depending on the activity, some things work better when scheduled weekly or bi-weekly. As with everything, it may seem like a lot of work at first, but once you put these ideas into practice, you'll have so much time left over and things will run smoothly. These are the different types of organizational tools and schedules that I use:

- Family monthly calendar
- Personal calendar
- Mom's schedule
- Kids' schedule
- Chore chart
- Family menu
- Grocery list
- Bills and budget spreadsheet
- Filing system
- To-do list

Personal Calendar

- You've already worked on your family's calendar. Since this unit is about YOU and how to take care of YOU, start by organizing your personal calendar. I personally like to print out my calendars, but I understand that some of you moms are more tech savvy and like to have your calendars on your phone and computer. Remember, this is about you and what works best for you. On this calendar, write down personal appointments, church activities, your husband's activities, date nights/sitter needed, birthdays, gifts you need to buy, phone calls you need to make, grocery days, holidays, recitals, competitions, rehearsals, music lessons, sports games, kids' extracurricular activities, errands, vet appointments, doctor's appointments, personal time, fun time, and vacations. Plan ahead!

- Mom's schedule: This schedule I do weekly. I have it ready to go by Sunday evenings and it spans from Monday to Friday. It goes hand in hand with my monthly calendar, but I use this schedule to organize what I need to accomplish on a daily basis. Don't go to sleep realizing you haven't done what's on your schedule. Do everything today and it will be easier tomorrow. Here is a sample of what it could look like:

Mom's Schedule

Time	Task
6 - 6:30 am	Devotion / coffee
6:30 - 7:00 am	Personal time / me time
7 - 8 am	Lesson Plan
8 am	Fix Breakfast
8:30 - 9 am	Breakfast / Family Worship
9:00 - 9:30 am	Clean up Breakfast
9:30 - 9:45 am	Prayer Walk
9:45 - 10 am	Lunch Prep
10 - 2:00 pm	Assist kids with school
2 - 2:30 pm	Lunch Set up
2:30 pm	Lunch
3:00 pm	Clean up
3:30 pm	Exercise / walk
4:00 pm	Shower
4:30 - 5:30 pm	House chores
5:30 - 6:30 pm	To do's / Must Do / Have to
7 - 8 pm	Lite Dinner
8 - 9 pm	One on one time
9 - 9:30 pm	Family Time & Worship
10:00	Prepare for tomorrow

- Keeping all charts, schedules, calendars, menus, grocery lists, and to-do lists visible makes it easier to keep track of what everyone is doing at all times. Accountability is very important for success.
- House chores: My house is tidy but not perfect, and I am okay with that. Training our children to help around the house and do their chores has been a part of the process since the beginning. They are responsible for their rooms, taking out the trash, and helping unload the groceries. We do not give allowances for chores since it is our home and it's everyone's responsibility. But we do have positive reinforcement rewards and incentives. Our household chores will look something like this: Everyone picks an area of the house to organize and tidy for 15 minutes. One room of the house gets cleaned daily. Fridays, floors get swept and mopped. The front and back porch get swept and cleaned, and the whole house gets tidied up for Sabbath. If your budget allows it, consider hiring extra help at least twice a month to do a deep clean of the house. It is well worth it. Deep clean one room a month, and the garage twice a year. We do this in spring and winter. Laundry is done on Mondays and folding takes place right from the dryer. Live a simple life. The more you have, the more clutter and the more cleaning. Once a month, we go through our closets and drawers, and we make three piles: donate, keep, throw away. We will donate to thrift stores, Goodwill, churches, charities, shelters, or a family we may know that is in need. Try not

to collect mail or too much paper. Each of my kids gets to keep a box per year of memorabilia and their school portfolio. They take pictures of special projects and everything else.

- Family menu - Meals at our home are very simple, but full of nutrients. Breakfast is important as is our late lunch, which takes place around 2:30. Later in the afternoon, the kids will have a light supper (sandwiches, raw veggies, smoothies, quesadillas) and cereal is always a nightly option. I follow the pyramid guidelines and formulate the menus with that in mind. Meals are planned for a period of two weeks and everyone gives their input on what they would like to eat. For the most part, I cook everything from scratch, even our almond milk (the Almond Cow machine is the best!). On Sundays, I set a portion of my time for meal prep. I freeze lots of things for emergency days. On a side note, I encourage you to try a new or different recipe every week. Everyone will love it. A tip for making mealtime prep fast and fun is having a potluck day. On this day, you can bring out all of your leftovers and it makes your lunch interesting and full of variety!

CRUZ FAMILY WEEKLY MENU   DATE:

MONDAY

Breakfast	Lunch	Light Dinner

TUESDAY

Breakfast	Lunch	Light Dinner
	TACO TUESDAY	

WEDNESDAY

Breakfast	Lunch	Light Dinner

THURSDAY

Breakfast	Lunch	Light Dinner

FRIDAY

Breakfast	Lunch	Light Dinner

SATURDAY

Breakfast	Lunch	Light Dinner

SUNDAY: EAT OUT!

- Grocery list - There is nothing more frustrating than to start cooking and realize that you are missing ingredients, or to feel like you just shopped for groceries but don't know what to cook. Time and energy get wasted this way. This is why preparing your grocery list based on your meal menus works so well. There are lots of staple items that we have at home because we use them daily (salt, onions, garlic, olive oil). There are others we buy on an as-we-need basis. The rest is bought according to what we know we are going to eat for the next two weeks. This helps not only to save time but also money. I love online grocery shopping, which has saved me from countless hours of store time, traffic time, and overspending. Pet supplies, cleaning supplies, washing detergent, bottled water, paper goods, and so much more are delivered right to my door. I keep this list handy and write down items that we are out of first. Then I fill in the rest as needed. Shopping becomes intentional and productive.

This list can help you:

Cruz Grocery List

DATE:

Fruits	Vegetables

Dairy	Grains

Desserts	Bread

Deli	Frozen

Snacks	Cereal

Cruz Grocery List   DATE:

Drinks	Baking

Canned	Pasta

Produce	Cleaning Supplies

Toiletries	Paper Goods

Condiments	Household

- Bills and budget spreadsheet - Living on a budget can be stressful and finances at times will become a big issue. Going from two salaries to one is not easy. I have experienced both sides of the spectrum.

Although I have my career, I chose to stay home and this necessitated a lot of financial adjustments. Sit with your husband and formulate a finance plan. Be conscientious of the fact that your household now runs on a one-salary income. It is not his or your money, just like it is not his or your household. This is a partnership, and everyone holds a different responsibility to make it work. I've known many families where the dad is the one who stays home, and it works just fine for them. I have loved being a stay-at-home mom, and I do believe that it is God's plan for mom or dad to stay home and raise the family. With that said, it is a privilege that comes at a price. Financial stability is important and planning even more so. Talk with your husband or with a financial expert and come up with a budget or a debt-free living plan that will benefit you and give you financial freedom. There are many books on this subject and many financial advisors willing to help. In the meantime, let me give you some strategies that will help you get started and guide you in the right direction. You want to know my secret for all these years? Tithe, yes, tithe! Simple as that. Malachi 3:10 says, "Bring the whole tithe into the storehouse, that there may be food in my house. 'Test me in this,' says the Lord Almighty, 'and see if I will not throw open the floodgates of heaven and pour out so much blessing that there will not be room enough to store it.'" My husband and I adopted this practice very early on in our marriage and I can testify that God has been good. Another practice we've adopted is being wise about how we spend our money. Here are some rules we guide ourselves by:

- Create a monthly bill chart
- Create a budget
- Live within your means
- Have a savings account
- Do I want it or need it?
- Never buy on impulse
- Return if not needed
- Vacation fund
- Shop on sale
- Be frugal
- Open junior savings accounts for kids

Unit 6: How to Keep It All Together

CRUZ FAMILY MONTHLY BILL CHART   DATE:

Bill/Payee	Due Date	Amount	Online/scheduled	✔

TOTAL AMOUNT DUE: TOTAL SAVINGS: TITHE:

- Filing system - Although I have gone paperless for many things, there are still important documents that are held in our possessions and that need to be in an organized place in our home. For this, I have three different organizing techniques that have worked very well.

File organization tip #1 - At the beginning of the year, I buy file cardboard and organize and label important papers for that year. The labeling machine is my best friend. Everything gets a label with name and year. You can customize them to match your family's needs. For my family, it would look something like this:

- Life insurance
- Property insurance
- Medical insurance/vision/dental/prescriptions
- Homeschool papers per child
- Pet info/vaccination card

File organization tip #2 - In a file cabinet, file important documents that do not change yearly. For example:

- Passports
- Birth certificates
- Marriage license
- Social security
- Living will
- Certifications
- Continuing education information

File organization tip #3 - Use a basket! In this basket, I drop anything tax related: receipts, letters, W2s. After talking to your accountant, make a list of receipts that you need to keep in this basket and put it all in there. Once a year, this basket gets organized and ready to hand over to your accountant.

- To-do list - This is one of my favorites during the day. I keep my to-do list very handy. Some of you might like to keep a magnetic list on your refrigerator instead and that is fine. I have opted for a notebook that I keep on my countertop. Every time I remember something I need to do, something I need to buy, a conversation I need to have with my husband, a bill that needs special attention, car maintenance, and so forth, it goes on the to-do list.

Use a method that makes your life simpler. I can only tell you what has worked for me and how all these tips and skills have allowed me to be more effective and productive during my day. This is the way I've been able to organize my life so I can better tend to what is truly important to me—my family and myself! You can also have a fantastic family, marriage, and kids. Most importantly, you don't have to do it alone. This book and this unit are merely a guide for what you can do if you really set your mind to it.

Challenges: Taking the Risk

I remember periods of my life when I was consumed by fear and anxiety because I felt as if I was not adequate for this job of homeschool mom. It seemed as if it was too much for me to handle. I sensed the criticism from friends and family members. Colleagues were doubting my decision. Gossip like, "Rebeca has gone mad for wanting to keep her children in a bubble" hurt me deeply. Comments like, "I would never do that to my children" were overheard as I attended social functions. I went from being accepted and loved to feeling like an outcast and very alone. But I was convinced that this was my life's calling. I had voiced it in prayer, and I knew that it was best for my family. Giving my children my leftover time, my minimum, my tiredness, my bad moods, my irritability, and my exhaustion from a long day at work was not what I wanted or what God wanted. I dreamed of a loving, peaceful home filled with laughter, curiosity, time well spent, hugs, snuggles, music, dancing, healthy meals, reading, sunshine, and happiness. And I was determined to make it so.

With all eyes on me, I emerged into a lifestyle that has become the biggest and most wonderful blessing and journey. The past 17 years of my life are worth repeating. If I had to do it all over again, I would certainly take the risk. I understand you are full of doubt, and maybe you wonder if it's worth it. You are anxious about the future of your children. You don't know how to start and what if you fail? What would people say? You've seen the positive effects homeschooling has on families. You like the idea, but you have limiting beliefs that stop you. You keep telling yourself that you can't make it on one income, when in reality you know that you can downsize, live with less, and pay off some debt. Prepare ahead of time. You tell yourself that you have wonderful public and private schools in your area. This might be true, but you're still not convinced that leaving your children in the care of that system is the best thing for your family and for their upbringing. People often ask you how your children are going to socialize and because you have not done all your homework, you stumble and start thinking that your kids will not be sociable. In reality, homeschooled children are very sociable, very outspoken, very sure of themselves, and very mature. You as the parent need to provide them with the necessary tools and the environment to acquire the proper socialization. There is a reason why you picked up this book. I have a success story and I am here to guide you, help you, and teach you how to do it as well. You, too, can have a success story.

Taking a risk is always frightening, and the limiting beliefs can sometimes be paralyzing. You start to believe your own excuses, which keep you from taking the next step. Instead of being a catalyst for your family, church, and community, you inhibit yourself and defer what could be a life-changing experience. Let me give you peace and encourage you to take the risk. You are not alone on this journey. Though there are many thoughts stopping you, I want you to know that there are people that have gone through this and paved the way so you, too, can do it.

Homeschool

It is very important to belong to a support group as parents of homeschooled children. It gives you a container that can help you hold these doubts. The support group my family joined had guest speakers, parents' success stories, question and answer sessions, fellowship with other homeschool families, and was a great way to stay informed of what was going on in the homeschool world. Our kids loved going because they would meet other children their age and made lots of friends. Where there is a will, there's a way. What is it going to take for you to have a "win" mentality?

Our children are very particular when it comes to that "win" mentality. All three have that attitude. They are very competitive, not for the sake of competing against each other, but for the sake of winning for themselves. We saw this character trait early on, and instead of discouraging it, we tried to modify the behavior so they could use it for good. For example, my husband and I decided that putting our son in community sports would do him good because he would have an outlet for that "win" attitude.

When competing, children have to face losing sometimes. But losing was not on my son's agenda. He was five years old when he started baseball and you would see him always striving to be the best. Even when his team would lose, he would have the most runs or strike the most batters out or win the game ball at the end of the game. He was always striving to win.

Our younger daughter also displayed this type of personality. We put her in soccer at a young age. Her team lost that season.

I remember her getting out of the minivan, and as she walked towards the house, she yelled at the top of her lungs, "I am the best loser ever," meaning she had won at losing!

Our older daughter would never give up. If she lost, she would not display a loser personality. She would immediately join in again and try until she won. Ultimately, you are competing with yourself to be better and to prevail over any challenge you face.

If by any chance my children faced a situation that brought them down, I would tell them they had five minutes to feel bad and after the five minutes were over, it was time to figure out what they could learn from it in order to do it better.

In homeschooling, you need to have a winner's mentality. There is no other choice, no other alternative, no second place, no maybes. You are in it to win it. A winning mindset will get you the results you want because there is no room to fail. You are not in competition with others, you are not competing with a system. You are in a winning mindset where you are on the winning team. Your family, your children, and your homeschool become what you are working towards. You're not better than someone else; you are not doing this to beat anyone or to prove to your peers that you can do it. They are not your challenge—you are!

Statistics change all the time and that is why I don't like to use them. I'd rather speak to you from my heart and my experiences, which to me have more validity. Although homeschooling has been legal in all 50 states since 1993, mothers continue to second-guess themselves and keep believing the lie that they are not good enough to teach their children.

Let me liberate you from the top four limiting beliefs that, in my opinion, might be stopping you from making this decision.

- Limiting Belief #1 - I am not a teacher. This is very common among first-time homeschool moms. You do not feel adequate enough to take on this responsibility. We all feel that way! Ironically, we went to school for 12 years and we feel incompetent to teach what we learned. Just because you are not an expert in a particular subject area does not mean that you can't teach your kids. Let me give you comfort in reassuring you that you don't need to know everything. There is no correlation between how well a homeschooler performs and the academic level of their parents. Thankfully, curriculums nowadays come with a teacher's or mom's guide and lesson plans for each day. There are tutors available, as well as videos online to assist you in the process. I'd like to share a story that may give you a different perspective on what a mother can do. As you read, remember that what we take to be our inadequacies might just be our biggest strengths.

    One day, Thomas Edison's teacher gave him a piece paper and asked him to hand it over to his mother. Thomas Alva came home, handed it to his mother, and asked her, "What does it say?" After reading the paper, Edison's mother started crying. When Edison asked the reason, she read the letter in a loud voice. "Your son is a genius. The school is not up to his caliber and we don't have the resources to hire teachers that can teach your son. Please teach him yourself." Thomas Edison's mother began to homeschool him in a way that supported his burgeoning interest in science. At age 10, he told his mom he wanted a science lab and she agreed. She spent all she had, and they built one in the basement. Some years later, his mom became ill and was in great pain. She needed surgery and was hospitalized. The surgeon told Thomas that the surgery needed to wait until the morning because there was no light. It was then that Thomas invented the light bulb. He tried 99 times, but on the 100th attempt he succeeded. One day while looking through his old family things, Edison saw a folded sheet of paper in one corner of the desk. To his surprise, it was that same paper that his teacher had sent to his mom. The paper read, "Your son is addled [mentally ill] and we cannot let him attend school anymore. He is expelled." Edison became very emotional and cried for hours after reading this paper. He wrote in his diary, "Thomas Alva Edison was an addled child who, by a hero mother, became the genius of the century." I don't need to convince you that you are the perfect teacher your child needs. You are more than capable and suitable. Thomas Edison's mom was not a teacher, yet her support and self-confidence in him gave him the tools he needed to change the world.

- Limiting Belief #2 - This is probably the number one question asked when others find out that you are going to homeschool. How are your children going to socialize? To socialize simply means to participate in social activities, mix socially with others, and make someone behave in a way that is socially acceptable. So, in fact, when people ask, "How are they going to socialize?" what they really mean is, "How are they going to make friends?" because you can teach socialization skills. I can teach my child how to speak, make eye contact, talk to others about their interests, and so on. Do you remember your teacher telling you, "You are here to learn, not to socialize?" Then why do people think that the only way a child can socialize is in a school setting? Socialization goes beyond that, and what schools offer in my opinion is forced socialization because children have no choice. Think about it. When you grow older, are you ever going to be in a college class where people are only your age? Or in a job where all the employees are your age? So how do we prepare our children for that eventual reality? Society says that in order for your child to fit the norm, they have to do the things that have always been done. For example, they might be expected to attend prom, ride on a yellow bus, or be a part of a student government. There are many solutions and options to facilitate these experiences:
  - Co-op group - find one to meet your needs or create one

- Church/Vacation Bible school - join one or start one
- Community service - it works well for older kids
- Public school extracurricular classes - our older daughter took guitar lessons in a public-school setting and participated in their music program
- Swimming program - our children participated in a park swimming summer program
- Summer camp - gymnastics and ice-skating summer camps are very popular among our girls
- Clubs/sports/band/debate teams/theatre/robotics

The beauty of the homeschool experience is that you get to pick and choose what you do and with whom you do it. Our children have experienced what it is like to ride in a yellow school bus, participated in a homeschool prom, and taken part in graduation. My children are not a product of data in and data out. They are better socialized as homeschoolers because all these things are possible. They are not confined to a structure dictated by taxpayer money. People have the misconception that all we do is stay home. They are not aware of the options. When I taught in a school, I had children in the school setting that were shy, introverted, and liked to be alone, yet they were in school every day. We are all different, yet we leave it to a system to decide. My children belonged to a homeschool co-op with children of varying ages, ranging from five years of age through high school. One day, as our children were playing basketball, one of the moms came to me and said, "My five-year-old son says that Jason (14 years of age at that time) is his best friend. I asked him why and he said, "Jason always lets me play basketball." Jason was not even aware, but every time little Matthew would come over to where the big boys were playing, Jason would let him throw the ball and the big boys would continue the game. This is exactly what it's all about—integration. No one feels left out because everyone matters, from the youngest to the oldest. This is socialization at its best. Our older daughter was able to go to college, live with a roommate she had never met before, do well in her classes, meet new people, acquire friends, and be a team player because she was well rounded in her socialization skills as a homeschooler. In addition, homeschooled kids "seemed to be more independent, creative and could connect the dots… And because they were not segmented by age in a classroom, they were comfortable carrying on a conversation with people of any age."[1] Homeschoolers are more likely to have higher self-esteem and be less susceptible to peer pressure. Isn't this what you want for your child?

- Limiting Belief #3 - Homeschooling is expensive. Like everything in life, you can make of homeschooling what you want. Although a homeschool room, manipulatives, computers, expensive curriculums, yearly passes to

---

1 Ramaswamy, Swapna Venugopal. "Out of the classroom: Parents explore home-schooling." *USA Today*. November 9, 2014.

museums, co-op groups, extracurricular activities, and field trips are all available, they are not necessary. Your homeschooling can be both simple and effective. We have based our lives on one income, and by doing so we have the freedom to educate our children. In reality, all you really need is a #2 pencil, paper, a library, a dining room table, and nature. Today, various resources, including free online programs and free curriculums, are available from your county. Museums, botanical gardens, theme parks, nature centers, and other venues have a homeschool program free of charge. You have the freedom to design the program that best suits you and your budget. You have only one requirement: You need to do your homework!

- Limiting Belief #4 - Homeschool is a religious thing. At one point, it was true that the majority of people would homeschool from a religious perspective. Many parents were critical and skeptical about schools using their platform to indoctrinate children. Therefore, families with more conservative viewpoints kept their children home to give them a more faith-based curriculum with biblical teachings. Although a good concept, homeschooling was widely criticized because educators felt that in doing so parents were keeping their children from being exposed to different walks of life. A lot has changed since then and although a vast majority of parents keeping their children home comes from a more holistic and Christian perspective, we cannot generalize and say that only Christians or faith-based people homeschool. Parents in general are searching for something different and homeschooling has become a vibrant, growing movement for all parents looking for options. Schools are doing the best they can, but they cannot give an individualized education like parents can. Another reason parents opt to homeschool is because their child may have a learning disability and they want to educate without the labels and medication often required in school settings. Another rising concern among parents is safety: drugs, peer pressure, cliques, rejection, sexual conduct, and bullying.

One afternoon, I was in a board meeting and my younger daughter, Melanie, had come with me. I asked her to stay in the lobby as I attended my meeting. Some other children were there, and they sat on the stair and started to talk. I came out periodically to make sure she was fine. She seemed good, talking and laughing as any seven-year-old would. That evening as I got home, I received a phone call from a mom of one of the girls who was with Melanie in the lobby earlier. I noticed sadness in her voice as she said, "Good evening, Rebeca, do you have a moment to talk?" "Of course," I replied, "Is everything alright?" She said, "Yes, I want you to thank Melanie for standing up for my daughter tonight. See, when we were at the meeting some other girls came over to drink water at the fountain and started to make fun of my daughter for being overweight. They giggled and mocked her. This has been going on for some time, not only there but at her school, and is causing her a great deal of pain.

But tonight was different. Melanie stood up to them and told them not to be mean like that. She said that God created them all to be different and that she was beautiful the way she was. And that if they did that again, she would tell on them." She went on to say, "See, my daughter is 12 years old and she has never had the courage to stop them from teasing her or bullying her. But tonight, Melanie did it. And we want to thank her." Where does a seven-year-old get the courage to stand up for what is right? Where do our kids become so secure in who they are that they are willing to defend other children against bullying and mistreatment? How do they get the strength to stand up for what they believe? I believe HOMESCHOOL is the answer.

ACTION STEPS

*"I am not telling you it's going to be easy,
I am telling you it's going to be worth it."*
—*Art Williams*

www.ingramcontent.com/pod-product-compliance
Lightning Source LLC
Chambersburg PA
CBHW020908080526
44589CB00011B/492